LOVING SOBRIETY

A REAL JOURNEY FROM ALCOHOLISM, ADDICTION
AND DENIAL TO RECOVERY, CONTENTMENT AND JOY
THROUGH THE TWELVE STEPS AND SOBER LIVING
MIRACLES

R.J. BOOTS

CONTENTS

INTRODUCTION

Remember when you were a kid, and everything was new?

Words were like puzzle pieces, and you didn't know where they fit.

Don't you sometimes feel like that puzzle piece that doesn't quite fit? I'm guessing; I know I do.

Sometimes I feel like a word looking for a sentence trying to make a paragraph to form a chapter to complete a book in someone else's story. It couldn't be my story! No Way! This turn of events is not how I outlined it when I was a kid.

But, I digress. When we were little, those adults sure got excited when we Babbled Ma or Pa, Momma, Dadda! When we crawled for the first time, their mind was BLOWN! We took a first Step --- they went freaking CRAZY!

We were Stars. We could almost do no wrong. We Crapped our pants - awe, so cute. Puked on the dog -- adorable! We didn't have a lot of rules, but they were terrified they would fail and let us perish while we were playing goo-goo gaga on the floor. They would do anything to keep us from going too far astray.

This all was new for them too. They were scared. However, they were right there to show us the ropes. Which took quite a while to figure out, but still, there they were to help.

We were little rebels then, too, weren't we? They say - don't mess with the cat - and we immediately yanked its whiskers and petted it backward! They say-Stay away from the stairs! We are performing a death-defying Balancing act on the ledge. She says Don't eat the ants! Gulp. Yikes! Aaaaaaaah !!!!

We didn't want to do everything they asked of us back then, either did we?

Or, some of you were perfect little Angels, huh?

You may have had a different story.

I was a perfect child and caused no issues, fuss, or stress. Except for almost dying from the umbilical cord around my neck at birth, almost checking out not breathing in the crib as a baby and having surgery for a blocked intestine at three months. Other than that- smooth sailing. Oh, the accidental baseball bat to the face at the hands of my brother's friend at 8 was fun. Parents' stress levels must have broken the dial sometimes, especially for the first of their kids when it was all new.

I was the youngest. I was an adventurous, shy kid but got into many interesting situations growing up. Some parents knew about, but not all I would ever share with them. That is for sure!

Man - we didn't appreciate how hard being a parent is when we were kids, did we?

My parents also had their hands full with my sister, who had diabetes since she was four years old, and two brothers who invented their challenges, being wild, adventurous, and rebellious.

I have learned from watching my parents and them dealing with our challenges, failures, and successes, and now having kids of my own - that parenting never ends, and neither does learning or challenges. No matter what, challenges never end.

I had good parents. They had their challenges too.

Despite my dad's struggle with alcohol for many years until he got sober- I did not have a "bad" childhood per se. I know many people did, and many have lived very tragic stories. We all have stories, and they are our own stories and very different - yet here we are, in some ways, in the same boat.

If you are reading this book, no matter what gender, color, nationality, or background you have lived, odds are you have had your struggles. You have had challenges. You eventually got to a place or are still in a place where mind-altering substances like alcohol or drugs gave you some relief, an escape route away from dealing with things you didn't want to deal with, and a vacation from feelings you didn't want to feel.

It seemed innocent at first-Just, a little break from reality—even a little fun.

Ok, let's Actually be honest -- it was a freaking LOT of fun sometimes. Oh, until it wasn't.

For me at one time, maybe now for you -- it is more like torture, dependence, and bondage. Or - it will be, not for all but for many.

How did this happen? Why us? Others can drink or use and not ruin their lives!

Can they? Maybe.

But - more importantly, we can't. Why? We may ask in dismay. We never planned for this to happen. Yet again- here we are.

In many ways seeking recovery or learning to cope and deal with life without those substances of choice for each of us is like being that kid again where everything is new. Even things we once knew or learned that seemed so easy became hard again—some things we must learn repeatedly. We may still feel like that puzzle piece that just doesn't fit.

I am not a Pastor, and I am not a scientist, doctor, or psychologist. I am also not God, a judge, a teacher, and not a Prophet or Savior. Could I be a teacher? Well, I can undoubtedly teach what NOT to do from experience.

I am not going to spew a ton of statistics, show graphs or reports or interviews with scientists or give a chemistry lesson or pretend I know the thoughts or history of every addict or alcoholic or what will magically cure everyone and make life perfect. Some things you know from experience and the wisdom we have learned from others who have had the same or similar experiences.

I will tell how I went from an active, curious, creative kid to an occasional partier, to a regular drinker, to a functional alcoholic, to a morning drinking, daily Lush that couldn't stop on my own, to a devious denial expert, to a humbler man in recovery to a peaceful, sober, busy, responsible, content, often joyful, productive, sober person. Miracles can happen.

I'll describe some of the journey and the things that helped and that I know to be true.

I don't personally know you, yet I know you well in many ways. I care about you, and I care more than you will ever know because, in some ways, I was you. I've been in many of the same situations, anyway.

I hope you find the freedom I found, and it is there for you.

I have been to some places you have been, and I have felt some of the things you have felt and cried at some of the things you have.

We are all so different, yet in many ways, the same.

We are just trying to make sense of the senseless, see the light in the darkness, feel understood when we don't understand, and be loved when we feel unlovable.

I am just another person that found myself in a place I didn't choose, where I didn't want to be, in way too deep, paying debts on the choices I shouldn't have made and hurting people I never intended to hurt.

I have learned, however, not to blame others and not to say – this was by no fault of my own.

Here's one of the complex parts. We must own our part in ALL things that went wrong but not live in guilt or shame or live in the past. It is quite a balancing act indeed.

This admission will take time, and this self-forgiveness will take work, but we can do this! Let's walk through some of this together.

My journey was quite long, and only sometimes on a straight path, following only some of the rules and suggestions. That is for sure.

I still had to be the rebel, and I thought I could fix things myself. Damn it! If I only knew then what I know now. But we can't change the past, and we must move forward.

Do you ever feel the same, like you will figure out how to fix everything yourself?

Let's explore that ambitious endeavor.

Shall we?

You don't have to do all the "research" that I did to have many years of sobriety that I have now finally. You don't. I am grateful I finally saw the light.

You can't "fix yourself." Everyone needs some form of help at one time or another, and I promise you, everyone. It may look a little different for everyone, but even the strongest of the "self-willed type" can be humbled and baffled by the burden of addiction.

Let's see how your journey to sobriety or that of a loved one will look.

I hope and pray that it looks like a great success and that this book helps you realize that you can do this too.

I am thrilled to be sober. As my parents passed away a couple of years ago, I was delighted to have been sober for the last several years of their lives and built back their trust, hope, and belief in me, and shared our love and gratitude.

I am grateful for them.

I dedicate this to those beautiful, wise, and caring people I got to have as parents.

Here we go, then.

1

BEST SLAYED PLANS

HOW DID IT ALL BEGIN?

I sn't drinking supposed to be just fun? It's just something everybody does growing up, or so we thought. It was at the center of high school parties and college parties, all fun, games, and excitement, Spring break, campouts, beach parties, after school football games, baseball, basketball games, proms, dances, or whatever activity it was; we must have some beers and wine coolers, (does anyone remember those?) or mixed drinks, perhaps, shots, beer bongs, all kinds of ridiculous drinking games. We said we were hanging out "watching movies" to our mom & dad. Right, uh huh. Sometimes someone had weed or even a little blow. We were experimenting, being teenagers.

Maybe this portrait is too mild and innocent.

I realize others had a very different story, a very different beginning, without the parties and fun and innocent experimenting. Some of your stories are filled from the start with abuse, neglect, yelling, arguing, pain, and perhaps divorce or estrangement. No experimenting was involved with your introduction to alcohol and drugs, and it was all around you. Addiction was a family business. Your introduction to using alcohol or drugs was an escape from drama, pain, and suffering from the start.

It starts in many ways or similar ways and manifests in different and progressive ways for all of us.

For some - it was just curiosity, having fun, and never expecting any consequences. For others, it was like a new friend. It unleashed our inhibitions and opened us up from our introverted, shy persona. It may have been that escape, and we were a different person with more confidence. For others still, it was like throwing gas on a campfire that burned everyone's eyes from smoke and singed their eyebrows. It was a dangerous mix from the word go.

For the "Angels," it may have just kept us mellow, calm, and peaceful and made our shyness less paralyzing.

However, it started and manifested; it was a way to change how we felt, acted, dealt, or did not deal with situations and feelings, and interacted with others and the world in general - We liked it. No, we loved it.

We may have perceived it to make it easier to pursue that overwhelming obsession to figure out the opposite sex and get them to believe that we weren't a shy, scared dork and that they needed to be with us. After all, it made us more confident, funnier, charming, and irresistible, right? We will have our delusions.

Another possibility is that you were using alcohol or drugs to forget terrible, cruel, and wrong things done to you by someone of the opposite or same sex that was older and took advantage of you. This may be something that you could never tell anyone and may not tell anyone for many years, if ever.

For me, it started at a party of my brother's when our parents were gone.

There, I tried beer for the first time. I was 12. I was also 12 when I got extremely drunk for the first time. There were some older kids I hung out with on our street. One stole some wine from his parents' stash, and we all went into a field behind our neighborhood. The world was different then. It was when we were outside all the time. We would go out or all over the place, and our parents would tell us, "Be home before dark." Sometimes that would happen. We would ride our bikes all over the place or explore the fields where there were orange groves and crops of various vegetables. Anyway, this time, this kid brought this enormous jug of wine. He said, "let's contest who can chug the most at once!" What a tremendous flipping Idea! So, we did. I don't know who won, but we all chugged plenty for our scrawny, weasley body weight. It didn't take long to kick in. We were riding our bikes down the street. We felt spectacular. It was amazing. Then, we lay in the grass before a neighbor's house looking up at the stars. It was beautiful. I felt great! Until I didn't. Then, the reality of our ignorance of BAC kicked in, and I did not feel well. My friend guided me home, and I snuck up to my room. Later, after I passed out, my friend got caught by his mom, and she made him come to my house and tell my mom, who proceeded up to my room to find me passed out and covered in vomit. What an introduction to my future friend, alcohol, huh? One might think that would scare me straight and keep me away from it, and it did for a while. Not too long. Next time we were just a little more careful.

So began years and years of alcohol becoming a big part of many activities and, admittedly, a lot of fun on countless occasions. The switch didn't flip to the real addiction and prizes that came with it for many years.

However we started, wherever we came from, whatever we did, whatever was done to us, and how we reacted to it, all brought us to right now, right here together in a way, trying to find a path to make our life better and so that of those around us may be a little better as well.

Sometimes we need to change where we go and who is around us, but we'll talk about that later.

Neither this book nor any other person on Earth can make our past change, can make us forget what we have done or what was done to us, or give us a total "Do Over" of our life to this point. However, everything we do now and in the future can change the trajectory in which our life goes from now on. Do the same old shit, get the same old results. Play the same stupid games and get the same stupid prizes. Hold on to the same regrets, grudges, and resentments - you will pay the same price you have been paying for being controlled and owned by them and prove that the definition of insanity in fact, is doing the same things over and over and believing that you will ever get a different result.

One may hear about a million quotes and cliches in any of the many paths one may take to recovery. Sometimes I think I will punch someone in the throat if I hear another cliche. However, I am very peaceful now and would never do such a thing. Ha! Besides, I have also learned that although some of these cliches are cheesy as hell, and we will surely get tired of them - Damn it, most of them are cliches because they are true.

So, here we go - the first cliche of the book, oh, besides the "definition of insanity" thing above.

(I will try to use them sparingly to avoid hostile reactions.)

This one from the AA Promises: We will not forget the past nor wish to shut the door on it. This is not so much cliche as it is truth and sound advice, and there are many similar sayings or cliches. Like - The past is something to LEARN from, NOT to LIVE in. Or - Those who don't learn from the past will repeat it.

All these things are true. We can't change our past, and it is done. We can't make it go away, but we shouldn't dwell on it or live as if it defines who we are, what we can do, or where we can go from this day forward.

There are many quotes and cliches from all kinds of recovery programs, from AA to Celebrate Recovery to Regeneration and many, many more. There are many Twelve Step programs, Holistic Programs, and other types of programs, and I will reference and touch on some of them within this book. They all have their sayings and methods and points of view, and most with the intention of helping another person like them find solutions and recovery and a pathway out of the habits and self-destruction that became a way of life for us.

What I am NOT going to do is tell anyone that there is only one method for every single person on Earth to recover from their affliction. Certain things about addiction are universal or relatively universal. However, we all have different stories, bodies, minds, physiology, will, and faith. I will not push one method or program over another, nor will I bash any program either. I have gotten much help, knowledge, and wisdom from more than one of them, even if it took me a while to let it sink into my thick skull. I think the 12 steps and AA were a true blessing to the world when there was nothing like it, especially in the secular world at the time to help people realize they were not alone in their need and desire to recover from their addictions.

I am also not a theologist and will not make this a "Religious" book either. Although, faith can have an immensely invaluable benefit in recovering from things that ail us all. I know it has for me. Do not despair. There is no judgment here, and there will be no saying that you must believe precisely in what I say or think, or you can't recover. That is just not true. However- I will also say that the idea that there is a "Higher Power" with greater power, knowledge, and wisdom than us wouldn't be a stretch considering all the trouble we find ourselves in while thinking we know it all and that we are the highest of all high powers. No? One does have to take direction from someone, and look where taking direction from only us landed us.

Bottom line - we are much the same but very different. We all have different origins and upbringings and different stories to tell. No matter how that story began, we can write or co-write the rest of the story and decide the trajectory for the rest of our lives. We may need help getting started but must decide how much we want it.

You Can DO this!

2

WRONG TURN AT ALBUQUERQUE

AND THE FLIP OF THE SWITCH

W here did the fun end and absurdity, wreckage, and pain begin?

For most of us, the "Fun" or at least the ability to drink or use while enjoying it and not yet experiencing the eventual, ever-growing consequences and progressive wreckage, regret, and pain it will one day cause lasted for years, maybe even decades. There may have been periods in between where we may have been distracted by other noble, less destructive endeavors, putting off the inevitable game-changing occurrence of the "flip of the switch." This is where the regular use becomes heavy, the heavy becomes constant, and the constant becomes ever-present and begins to affect every single part of our lives. Addiction becomes real, and it is both mental and physical.

This is where it starts not to be fun at all, and we start to do things, say things, act in ways, and hurt others as we could never have imagined that WE would ever do. We may have even promised at a time - I would never be like that person or those people. We may have repeatedly promised that and meant it 100 % every time we said it. Yet again, here we are.

My dad was first a workaholic. He worked, traveled a lot, and achieved many things; he started his own business and found success. He provided well for us. We weren't rich, but we didn't lack anything we needed. There was a point where he started to celebrate that success. He deserved it, after all. He also began to drink. While I had great parents, and we did many fun things when I was young, there were many years when much of my memory of my dad was either working, playing golf, asleep or passed out on the couch after he got home. For years and years, every occasion involved him drinking. When I started driving, I sometimes had to pick him up at the golf course when he was drunk. It wasn't fun nor a pretty sight. I did make that promise. I said I would never get like that. I would never be an alcoholic, and I would never put my kids through that.

Never! I believed it every time I said it.

After years and years of him drinking like that, one day, my sister, my brothers, my mom, and I noticed, what the hell, Dad isn't drinking. It was like a miracle. He made a decision and stuck to it for over 34 years until the day he died. He came to me when he noticed I had a problem and introduced me to a friend who had quit after his "good influence" inspired him to stop. My dad thought that maybe I would like to talk to him. Imagine that. There are miracles. I did meet with that guy. Oh, I was drunk when I did it, don't be crazy. I had to calm the nerves, of course. There was no instant Miracle cure for me right then. He tried. It was a valiant effort. I will say he did begin a "curiosity" with this idea of Recovery. It didn't stick right then, though. It would take many years of denial before that kind of Miracle. But remember, I was never going to be like that. Sound familiar?

Regardless that I wasn't ready then, I am still grateful to that man because he did plant a seed. It would just take a lot more "research" on my part personally to make that poor seed grow.

The "flip of the switch" didn't come for me until after all the years in high school, many wild times in college, after living away from home in the fantastic, crazy city of Hollywood, California, meeting rock stars or wannabe rock stars and partying like crazy. Then I moved away from there and "settled down" a bit. Still, there were many years of playing on a softball team and golfing and drinking afterward. Heavy drinking was regular, but the "Switch" still hadn't flipped into a full-blown addiction. Oh, I was working up to it. This inevitability probably started in that field when I was 12 and later when drinking relieved my shy kid's inhibitions. It is a progressive affliction, after all. Some people that drink regularly don't fall into it; some don't succumb to it. More do in one way or another than one might think, however.

Then, I met my future wife. She had never drunk a drop or done a drug in her entire life. Not even once! Can you believe that? Where do they make these people? Do people like that even exist? A person like us might ponder. They do. There are much more of those that live full-time in reality than we think, and my wife is one of them. How could this work? That is a question I still wonder. How did I pull that off? Holy Frijoles. Sainthood. She is a Saint.

But wait, if she is such a good person, how could she be or stay with an addict? Addicts are all bad people with no morals that have no worth or purpose and ruin everything they touch and don't care about anything or anyone but themselves! Isn't that what many believe?

OK - now let's wake up from that sad delusion. While I do not claim to be the most remarkable, most noble, flawless person around, I know that I am not a "bad person" and never was. Neither are you, right? You would realize if you were.

I made plenty of mistakes, and mistakes are innately human and primarily worthy of forgiveness. For the most part, they are not a searing hot irreversible brand of a "bad person."

There are no perfect people on this planet, but I know for a fact that a good percentage of people with addictions are wonderful people. Further, I know firsthand that many people in Recovery are some of the kindest, most forgiving, humble, diligent, hard-working, hopeful, faithful, and trustworthy people one can be blessed to know. All are broken at some point, but there is indeed hope for the broken. I promise there is.

So, one may think my lovely wife's influence would settle me down and get me to drink normally or quit. Nope. Yes, I changed my ways for a while to not blow up our marriage right away, somewhat at least. OK, not much improvement but some. Mostly, I just began hiding how much I was drinking. So, I thought anyway. Whenever we think people don't know what we are doing, newsflash, they usually know, or they will begin to figure it out eventually. We are so clever, we think.

My" switch" flipped a couple of years after I married this wonderful person who must be a saint to still be with me after the journey we embarked on.

I know it doesn't always happen that way, and I am grateful every day to have survived and with her by my side.

I cannot promise, nor would I ask, an alcoholic or addict to expect that everyone they want to will stay with them through their struggles. It often does not happen, and that would be a false promise. We all will experience loss, and I certainly did in other ways. I promise, however, that we can get through it, survive, recover, and pave the way to happiness and joy if we don't give up.

While I can say that I was sort of what one might call a "functional" alcoholic for many years, I held a job, didn't get divorced, nor lost my kids that we would eventually have together. I realize I am lucky in that sense, and many people can't say that and have lost everything.

There is no sense, matter, or worth in comparing whose bottom is worse. Here was my story; you have yours, and others will have theirs. Wherever we got to the bottom, it was somewhere we did not want to be. We might look up one day in a hotel, a hospital, or a detox center and sit there saying, "how the F did I get here?" We can't even believe it.

I believe I had many bottoms. As they say, we must get rid of the shovel to keep from digging the bottom deeper. Or, every time I thought I hit bottom; a trap door went down farther. By the time I finally got rid of the shovel and embraced Recovery more seriously, I had been "trying out" this recovery thing for years.

I had many close calls along the way. Once, I was taken to the hospital with a .40 Blood Alcohol level. I drank down a bunch of 100 Proof Vodka too fast to finish it before my wife got home. An average person may have been dead. I was up and around walking through the hospital and released after refusing to stay within hours. The nurses may have thought, how is he walking? I had also crashed a car while falling asleep at the wheel. I had one DUI and narrowly avoided more many times. I was in detox centers seven times. It was often just a temporary respite, followed by half-measured attempts to stay sober, go to meetings to appease loved ones, and then right back at it, trying to be "discrete this time." I was going to do it my way, in My time. We all like to say that.

The important thing, however, is not how far we fall; it is how we rise from these places we have found ourselves, these places of despair and disbelief. However low our bottom is, it is the worst of us. It is embarrassing, shameful, demoralizing, and pathetic. It can seem very dark, and it may seem unimaginable that we ever got there.

I certainly got to a place I never imagined I would and did things I never imagined I would find myself doing to perpetuate my addiction. Lying to those I loved was a common practice. We don't want to be, but addicts are ALL Liars. Ever find yourself lying even though it makes you look and feel horrible? Never, right?

Regardless of the depth of my bottom, it was far enough, and no question that losing everything, including life, was an impending possibility. I can tell you with 100% certainty that the "switch" did flip. I had become a daily, drink-in-the-morning, hangover-rebuking, physically addicted alcoholic.

Today, I do not let the word, Alcoholic define me, as I don't believe it is who I am but -an affliction I have. But at that time, I was certainly physically and mentally addicted. Like anyone in such a position, I did some genuinely embarrassing, demoralizing, dangerous, and sometimes utterly ridiculous things during these years - as any addict worth the badge of such insanity has done. I will touch on some of those later.

I aim to offer hope and possibility for anyone who works at it and doesn't give up on recovering and finding joy than tell crazy, embarrassing stories in a drunkalogue. However, some reference to where one will go, places we will find ourselves, the pain we will cause, and the wreckage we will leave in our path also have a valuable purpose in showing from what depths one can go, emerge from, achieve Recovery, and live to tell the tale and help others to do the same in the end as well. One of the best rewards in Recovery is sharing wisdom and giving hope to others. Some might even say that is a moral requirement, and it does help you as much as it will help them.

No pressure. No rush, and let's take this methodically. Patience truly is a valuable virtue.

Moving along, what is this "switch" I speak of you may ask.

When I say, "flipped the switch," - I am not referring to the gradual progression into addiction. A flip occurs, and we don't get to the bottom overnight. Here, I am referring to an actual period when there is a physiological change in our body. There is a point where along with the mental obsession to drink or use, a physical craving and an actual change in the body's chemistry also occur. I know it because I can clearly feel it.

There was a time before the "flip" that we could drink and have a few, not drink for a while, maybe not even get hangovers. We could have a few drinks on the weekend, go to school, work, and go along with life, and there was not such an obsession. However, once we have this physiological change in our body, the reaction to alcohol when we drink is different. Once we get to this point, we are usually never stopping the drinking cycle. However, if we stop for a while and then drink, the obsession, the need, and the unquenchable desire for more kick in. I won't say you can't just have one. You can never again have one without this craving and obsession kicking in. Your body has changed, and it doesn't change back. You may have a couple of drinks, get away with it, and thus a month later or even years later, say, hey, that last time wasn't so bad, I can do it again. Then, you will have a few drinks, next time 4, 6, 10, and so on. It is a lie we will tell ourselves over and over - that if we got away with it once, we could do it again. You can't. There are always anomalies, but for the most part, a true alcoholic can't. We must give up that fruitless, self-destructive, and never rewarding delusion and lie that we can ever drink like a "normal person" again if we want to recover and have a good life.

Again, I am not a scientist. I am not basing this on a cache of compiled, complex data. I am basing it on personal experience, lots of physical "research," and countless relapses. Does that make me an expert? It makes me an expert in my experience, journey, and testimony. That's it. However, I also gathered testimonies, much wisdom, experiences, stories, revelations, practices, and principles, and witnessed miracles of countless others along this journey I have also lived. You may say you are just one person, and it could be different for me. OK. Everyone is free to try it. But also try sobriety. If you want your old life back after testing this, you can pull down your big bottle from the shelf and all the same prizes and wreckage that came with it and carry on.

To make another humble plea to you again, however, I also have the backing, documented stories, and testimonies of millions of drunks and addicts that will tell you the same thing. Further, there is a great letter called "The Doctor's Opinion" that is in the forward of the "Big Book" of Alcoholics Anonymous that talks about this phenomenon of "craving" that we will get when we become addicted to alcohol. This doctor describes what I call "flipping the switch" into physical addiction as an acquired or developed "allergy" to alcohol. This doctor studied thousands of cases of alcoholics and found much evidence of this "phenomenon of craving," which occurs after we have the first drink, and the "allergy," which happens in the process of our addiction to alcohol. He also determined alcoholism was a "spiritual malady" that required a spiritual solution. I genuinely believe this, and I can certainly attest to his conclusions about the physiological aspect of addiction and I believe the Miracle of the spiritual as well. While this "allergy" to alcohol will never go away once the "switch has flipped "and will always recur no matter how long we "take a break" from alcohol, we can recover and experience a new "Psychic Change" which will eventually take away the desire and obsession to drink or use. We aim for this. That is the Miracle one must have the patience, dedication, and perseverance to experience.

Cliche alert: Don't give up before the Miracle Happens. Just don't give up.

3

ME? HAVE A PROBLEM? WHAT PROBLEM?

YOU HAVE A PROBLEM!

There comes a time for all of us when we begin to have some clues that our drinking or use of mind-altering substances is possibly not "normal." We figure out it may be causing some problems in our life. It usually takes longer for us to notice this than for others to see it. For some, hiding it to an extent is still possible. For others, we might as well have a tee-shirt printed with the phrase- Hi, I am an alcoholic/addict but don't tell anybody. Perhaps it is more a matter of admitting it that is the problem. By the time we accept it, it usually has progressed to the point that quitting is not a simple matter and will require work and help.

Therein lies the first hurdle to overcome. Almost nobody wants to admit they have such a problem and can't control it. They certainly don't want to admit they need help. Some reasons for this are embarrassment, shame, or fear of consequences. Another reason with perhaps even more weight is that we don't want to quit. Let's be honest. We love it. Or, at least, we did love it. We were able to drink or use before, and it was fun. We didn't cause any problems. We did it before; we can do it again. We don't want to HAVE to quit, especially on terms not controlled by us. We think there must be a way to control ourselves, avoid harmful consequences, and still drink or use when we want to, at least on special occasions or days ending with-DAY. In our mind, of course, we don't need help; we don't have a problem. We can quit whenever we want. We will stop one day. Maybe next week! Oh, wait, there's that wedding next week, then the reunion, and then the Super Bowl. But, the week after that, for sure! Yes, of course, uh huh.

I had countless occasions of "toning it down" or quitting for a while. The first was to see if I could not drink for 30 days. I Passed with flying colors. The celebration after that accomplishment was always quite a party. We had to make up for the lost time. I recall getting trashed after a softball game after that stretch. Next time will be different, and I will keep it mellow—famous last words.

The problem is, as we continue trying to make excuses, justify, deny, and take many half measures to "control" drinking or using, the signs of the problem and the consequences keep growing.

Many signs may indicate that we could have a problem or already be thoroughly addicted, and it may not be so blatant in the beginning. Here are some of the signs; loved ones might also take note.

We may start to drink when we don't plan to. This may frequently happen, even when we have important things to do. We might stay out extremely late regardless of something you must do the next day, and we fail to remember to do important things. We may stay somewhere longer and drink and then must try to act sober when we get to where we are supposed to go next. That usually fails, but WE think it went great.

We start missing things and appointments because of drinking or using and make all kinds of creative excuses because we couldn't make it.

We start to find more excuses to drink. Good times, we must celebrate! In sad times, we must commiserate over drinks. Feeling stressed – we must wind down and take the edge off. Feeling tired - a few drinks will help us sleep. If depressed, drinks will numb those feelings. If it didn't work; then another will make us forget. Missed an appointment or family gathering - oh well, effed it up already, may as well get toasted. Got fired - screw them, drink. Oh no, I don't have a job. I'm so bummed out - Cocktails! Wow- lots of time on my hands; I might enjoy it for a while and then look for another job. The bills can wait a little bit.

We also started to sneak drinks before, during, and after events. We must warm up with a few drinks before drinking, so people don't see how much we drink. We may smuggle alcohol into places. I cannot count the times I did that. Movies, meetings, at work, even Disneyland, the happiest place on Earth! I often had to sneak it for sure when others thought I quit so they don't think I have to drink everywhere I go. Oh, but I did. I would sneak off to "go to the bathroom" and run to the car to get a hidden stash. Devious and sneaky we are.

Drinking or using might start to magnify our feelings. If we are happy, we might get very exuberant. We might get very, very uptight and overwhelmed if we are stressed. If we are sad, we might get inconsolable. If we are depressed, we might get paralyzed with despair, fear, doom, and gloom. We might also have persistent and wide mood swings. Addiction is well-progressed when we find drinking or using is the only solution to these problems. It is certainly NOT the solution to any of them, so the issues pile up.

Relationships will start to suffer for many reasons. One reason is that we will start caring more about drinking and using than we do about nourishing relationships with our presence and care. It doesn't mean we don't love our friends or family; we will become less capable of showing it because our mind and body are over-taken with an obsession we can't control. To them - it may seem that we don't care about them. You know it is not the fact, but when we don't answer calls, don't show up, and aren't there when they need us - what would you expect them to think? They may also become devastated witnessing how we have changed.

Here is one of the most complex parts of addiction and relationships. A common reaction by relatives or friends is the perception that we don't care. The truth is that we care more than they ever know or can even understand. Certainly, someone that has never been addicted or experienced it firsthand cannot comprehend this or what it is like. They just can't.

They might think they can. They might believe they understand what is going on. It seems it is all our fault, and we are selfish and don't care about anyone but ourselves. They see us as a total F-up, ruining our life, being an a-hole, and neglecting our family and friends. In our mind, however, we have no intention to do that. We do love them, which is why this burden of addiction is like torture. We become stuck in a vicious cycle. We never intend to do bad things or hurt anyone, but we don't know how to stop doing the things that cause us more problems, and that does hurt people that we care about and care about us.

There is a scripture — Romans 7:19, that basically states:

> "I don't do the good things I want to do. I keep doing the evil things I don't want to do."

> — NIV

We enter a vicious cycle, and this is addiction.

We think we have control when we don't. We still believe we have control until perhaps restrained in a hospital bed, so we don't keep doing more stupid shit.

Long before that point, here are some other fun things that will happen in our lives or may have already happened. As one thing after another starts to unravel like a thread from a sweater, first slowly, then swiftly, we become overwhelmed at how to put things back in order. Keeping things in order, remembering things, and keeping track of what we said to whom and what lies we have told may add to the feeling of impending doom that becomes harder and harder and more prevalent.

We start to feel like we are just wasting our life. All these ideas, hopes, and dreams we had have been pushed farther and farther away to the point they may eventually seem inconceivable. But, we know, one thing that can make us forget about that for a while is more booze or drugs.

Early on, even when "partying" seems fun, we may get a glimpse into our choices that lead to procrastination and putting everything off. For example, we may ask ourselves, should I do schoolwork or go out and smoke weed and have some beers? Or - should I do more research on my dream career and start practicing it, or should I go bar hopping and wake up on a bench at the beach with seagulls pecking at my forehead? Or - I love writing and want to be a writer. Should I write or go with that friend to Tijuana and get trashed and thrown in jail?

Don't get me wrong. There is nothing wrong with youthful adventures, preferably ones not involving jail, but if our choice is ALWAYS to choose to party above all else and even the things we aspire to do one day - It might be a Red Flag for the future. It is always good to think further about the effect and consequences of ALL actions. As we sometimes say in Recovery - "Play out the whole tape" in your mind before you decide to do something consequential. (Not just the preview)

Spoiler Alert: The evil one makes the preview to entice us. The movie doesn't end how we plan.

Another ominous sign that things have gone too far, and addiction has set in is the dreaded drinking in the morning. You have heard of the hair of the dog or the feeling that the only thing that could cure the hangover, the throbbing eyeballs, headache, major battle going on in your stomach, and the hair-trigger gag reflex is, of course, another drink. "But it's just a Bloody Mary" it's got vegetables. It's good for us too! This can happen on vacations; it happens after parties. It happens with "normal drinkers" even. But it doesn't happen daily, weekly, or regularly unless there is a problem.

Drinking regularly in the morning to cure a hangover or to "get well" is one of the threshold signs in any list that people use to Question, "do I have a drinking problem" or "Am I an Alcoholic"?

Drinking in the morning regularly is like graduation to full-on addiction.

Most people who drink to any extent have had a hangover once. Some people have one once, and it's enough to convince them never to drink too much, or two, only have 1 or 2 glasses of wine or whatever, or not to drink. Sometimes people NEVER get hangovers. Sometimes people never get hangovers until their tolerance gets so high that they ALWAYS drink too much, and every morning their poor body screams from every living cell WTF did you do to me AGAIN, MORON!!!

When one begins to drink in the morning, it is because our body is sick. What should we expect when we put a gallon of poison into it? We are dehydrated. Our Blood sugar is through the roof. FYI, alcohol and alcoholic drinks have shite loads of sugar, and last I checked, downing loads of sugar is unhealthy for us. Further, we often don't eat when we drink a lot, so we are imbibing empty calories, tons of sugar, and poison (alcohol). It does not make for a bright and shiny morning.

When I was drinking, this was one of the worst parts. Not only did the alcohol ruin my sleeping pattern, the feeling in the morning and the obsession it created to make it stop were unbearable. People at first will think that alcohol "helps you sleep." If you have a small portion, maybe it makes you sleepy, and you go to sleep. Once addicted, however, we sleep horribly because our body is constantly screaming for more alcohol and more sugar. We can't sleep. Thus, we get the joy of lying there with the regret, shame, fear, and hopelessness committee having a conference in our head. We may try listening to all kinds of meditations or music or try over-the-counter reme-dies, but we still can't sleep. After we finally do sleep for a while, the cycle starts all over, and we must get more alcohol to "get well." That pain and the horrible sick feeling keep many of us continuing to drink and relapsing even when we wish we could stop. It is horrible and debilitating. It is not unlike an addiction or withdrawal to heroin or opiates in that way, feeling the overwhelming craving and the need to "get well." Surprising to some, with alcohol even more, though - just cutting off it too suddenly can be even more dangerous, causing seizures and even stroke or death in extreme cases. Fun stuff one learns in Detox.

I can't count the times when I had to "call in sick" or have an extended leave from work for "personal reasons" that my wife would get up to leave for work, and I would plead with her to stay with me even though I knew she had to go. Of course, it was a sad sight for her. Remember again that she is a saint to have stuck with me to help me through all this even though the vicious cycle and pain lasted years. Indeed, it made her sad. Many amends were due to her. It was painful and pathetic, but I just wanted her to lie there with me and put her arms around me because it was the only thing that made me feel any comfort, except for another drink which I would quickly retrieve the second she had left.

Sometimes, she took my keys, wallet, cards, license, and cash so I wouldn't drive or buy alcohol. I always had another card or stashed money and always had my ways.

We are devious to a fault.

One time when I went to the hospital and was on an IV and waiting until they checked me into Detox, I coerced my wife when she had to go to work that I needed my license and card for the charges at the hospital. Sounds reasonable. That wasn't why, though. The minute she left, I put on a jacket, sweats, and shoes, snuck out of the hospital with the IV tube still in my arm, walked down the road to a CVS, bought a bunch of little wine bottles, and chugged them in the bathroom. I returned to the hospital as nurses, and a security guard greeted me, asking where I went. I said I needed to walk around the hospital and stretch my legs. Whether they believed me is up for debate. I felt decent for a while as they checked me into Detox until I did not feel anything resembling decent.

The withdrawal from alcohol is a nightmare, so we will do bizarre, ridiculous, and foolishly creative things to get what we need.

Disclaimer - once again, I am not a doctor. Alcohol addiction is a severe, life-or-death matter. Detoxification from alcohol may require medical intervention and guidance. I make no recommendations on how individuals should detox from any substance. I only know this from my experience and the information I have learned in Recovery or from health institutions or books. I would advise seeking medical care or advice when attempting any form of Detox.

Isn't it amazing, though, that with all the horrible consequences and the possibility of loss, broken relationships, lost jobs, disappointed loved ones, and potentially life-threatening results of our actions, how we still hold on to the idea that we can control this and still drink or use, or we genuinely believe we can stop it alone with no help. As they say - it is baffling.

Here are a few dire reasons over the years I should have quit sooner but didn't or couldn't.

There was a point, or many when I quit for a while, so when I told everyone, I had stopped, I couldn't drink in front of anyone I knew because then they would know. So, I mostly drank alone.

I had friends that quit after my "good influence of quitting." They stayed sober, and I did not.

Everyone in my family knew I had this problem and always worried about me.

Once, about 20 years ago, I was in Palm Desert, California, to play this three-day Golf tournament with my dad. It was a big deal for me. We did great on the first day. I went out that night to a casino. Heading back, I fell asleep and drove off the highway going 70 miles per hour into sand dunes and got stuck for hours. Somehow, I did not get hurt. I drank again while stuck off the road in the dark in the middle of the night. Brilliant!

I predictably got spotted by the police, arrested, and ruined my rare opportunity to play with my dad in this tournament as I was in jail until the next day. That was a rough one to overcome, and it had been so important to me to do that with him. We commonly ruin important events or occasions when we choose our actions poorly and don't "play the tape through." I was lucky to be alive and not mangled against a guard rail or bridge pillar or to have killed someone. Concurrently, this was when my wife was pregnant with our first child too. Spectacular.

Another time I "quit" was when I volunteered to donate a kidney to my Diabetic Sister, that was on Dialysis. My two brothers and I all matched. I will only get a little into how I decided to jump in and do it. However, I will Inject one bit of how this molded my Faith even though the quitting didn't last once again. It was a somewhat scary thing, just the thought of someone going in and removing part of one's body. Thinking about it, I would feel nervous and a little sickish. I would get a sick feeling, not because I didn't want to do it. I did want to, and I loved my sister. The amazing thing was that I decided to stop drinking because of this. One day I was pondering it and just praying about it and that it would all go well. I asked God to relieve me of the fear. Take it for what you will. The fear immediately left me and never returned even months later until they knocked me out for the surgery. I was at total peace and had no fear. I have also had less fear about just about everything since then. Also, that kidney lasted over 17 years, giving my sister a new lease on life until she sadly passed at 53 due to other complications of her Diabetes and other health reasons.

My sister also had addiction issues, even with Diabetes but had been sober from drinking for over 20 years. This revelation of Faith would shape my life, yet it did not keep me from returning to the vicious cycle of drinking. However, planting seeds is valuable. We are still determining how long they will take to grow, but when you become aware they are growing, we are making Progress. Growing is good.

Cliche Alert: Recovery is about Progress, not perfection. Progress takes time, patience, and perseverance. Perseverance may be primary, as it is an arduous journey of missteps and mistakes. It doesn't have to be, but it usually is. Never giving up is the only way one can avoid failure. We never fail until we stop getting up. I promise the miracle is possible, and the rewards are great. Just don't give up!

There were countless other times I "quit." However, it wasn't until I finally stopped listening a voice that would always say, "One Day, if you take a long enough break, you can go back to having a drink , every once in a while," that I was relieved of it. Every time I quit, I always believed I was quitting for good. However, I always heard that voice, "someday it will be different." Whenever I thought that "break" was long enough, the voice got louder, and I would justify proving the definition of insanity once again.

I won't list all the "quitting," relapses, and stories. There were enough with similar results and always a similar outcome.

Let's get into how we can make Progress and quiet that voice. I hope this plants seeds.

I know for many like me; however, there is much more denial before the seeds start to grow.

We can think of a million reasons we are NOT like THOSE People and why we are different. Right?

4

BUT I AM NOT LIKE "THOSE PEOPLE"

THEY ARE LOSERS, SLACKERS, AND AMATEURS

M any have specific images that come to mind when they think of what is or who is an addict or alcoholic. Often the picture is a stereotype; the image is of a homeless person rummaging through trash cans and drinking from a paper bag or a strung-out junkie begging for money with deep dark eyes and tracks on the arm. Perhaps lots of tattoos come to mind. Face tattoos. Not to judge or disparage anyone with any tattoo. They are much more common now. Some of my good friends have tats and family too. There are plenty of fine-tattooed pastors and people from all walks of life. I am just speaking of reasons people might judge and perpetuate stereo-types. This may have been an image people picture. While many do know the actual image of who an alcoholic or addict is because they know them well, some still think of the stereotype.

The Truth is, however, that so many people know the real story because they live it. It can be anybody. It can be the mean abusive dad or the hardworking, loving dad that got hooked after just "winding down" with a couple of drinks after work or drinking with the softball team or golf buddies too often. It could be the mean, strict mom or the kindest, loving mom that just let those glasses of wine with the girls become too frequent. It can also be an accident or injury where we are trying to "ease the pain" with alcohol, or a prescription was given, used, abused, and gradually we got the bonus of addiction. It can start in many ways for anyone. It is our friendly neighbor. It can be our brother or sister, lawyer or doctor, accountant, or dentist, and it may be our teacher or even a Pastor.

Most of them are good people. Many of them are super bright and are very "functional" for a very long time without most people even knowing their struggle when they don't have to paint on a smile for clients, friends, family, or customers. They are just like you and me, whether you know it, believe it or not. There is a lot behind the "masks" we sometimes wear in public around others.

For millions, addiction is an insidious thief of joy, hope, trust, treasure, jobs, relationships, and life. The qualifications to join the "fun" have a low bar and can affect anyone. Some seemed predictable or obvious candidates for addiction and may spiral out of control in the open for all to see. Some are suffering in the shadows, faking happiness yet sinking gradually into this abyss of isolation, loneliness, and despair.

It is not a surprise when the obvious ones succumb to addiction. They indeed would have won the "most likely to be an alcoholic, drug-addicted disaster" if there were such a prize. It is also not a big surprise to hear of yet another rock star dying too young from addiction. Still, some of them survive and have inspiring tales to tell us. However, it might be more of a shock when people discover that the Prom Queen, Top Jock, or Valedictorian struggles with addiction because they seemed to have it all figured out and were so "perfect" before. Nobody is perfect. Most everyone has burdens and secrets, and often, not many know of them.

It is not unique to the stereotypical addict. It happens every day to people we may never suspect.

The fact that people do have stereotypes for addicts and that there is still a stigma and judgment (Often hypocritical) from some people towards them is yet another reason we may not seek help. We often feel shame and embarrassment for one. Further, again we fear that opening up about our struggle would mean that we would be potentially committing to stop drinking or using. We are not yet ready to do that now, are we? "Ready" is a relative term.

We think, whoa, Nelly! Wait a minute now. That is going way too far. I only want to tone it down! I don't need to quit entirely, like forever! I want information, not any commitment. I will look into it, but I'm good. I got this. Thanks anyway.

Here are just more of the many reasons or justifications that we will conjure up in our genius brain to not seek any help for the struggle we are NOT having. (In our mind, we are not struggling) No, we are just taking a little longer than expected to figure it out. Then, as soon as we figure it out, we will also solve all the problems for everyone else, tell them how we did it, and cure them too. Oh, and cure world hunger, cancer, peace, and every other problem because we are smart like that. We, however, need to be "Ready."

Thus, all these places people go that ARE struggling, like AA, Celebrate Recovery, Church, a counselor, a psychologist, or whatever, are certainly NOT for you or me. They are full of Losers, Slackers, and Amateurs! So, we think.

Ok, our Hubris might not go that far as to think we have ALL the answers, but close. It will surely go far enough to keep us from "Stupid Recovery meetings." Well, until that's the only place left to go.

We may still go, but; only to appease someone else or look like we are doing something to change, so friends and family don't give up on us.

The ego is a dangerous thing. Seriously.

Often in our mind, we are defensive because of our ego, paranoia, and commitment to "keeping appearances" that we have things under control and will figure things out on our own. Thus, whenever someone expresses concern for us or offers suggestions, help, or resources, we may feel that what they are doing is just getting in our business and that they are just prying and judgmental. We don't want to be rude, and we can't help but be defensive because our fragile sense of self, our retaining our independence, and sticking to our story that "All is Well" builds a wall to defend against all such attackers and do-gooders.

Our stubbornness and fear of change often cause us to rebuke offers of help. We may know we need it. We might even feel desperation. Admitting we have such a problem and especially agreeing to quit is another fear-inducing and overwhelming thought that makes us refuse what we desperately need. We may offer platitudes like - thank you for caring. I'll be ok. I'll look into it. Let's get a drink, Oops, I mean coffee sometime, ha-ha. For sure, I'm there, let's do it, penciled in, on the calendar, looking forward! With the fear of THAT subject coming up again, that meeting with this friend may never happen.

My dad approached me and asked if I had a problem after some time as it became more evident. Of course, he knew, having been there himself. He had been sober for years at this point. This was one of those points where one knows the jig is up, and there is no denying it. As much as we want to crawl away and avoid reality once again when one is confronted like this by a very smart, wise person with experience who we love and care about, words are hard to conjure.

We are used to lying and having people go along and accept what we say, usually feeling hopeless, sadly knowing we are lying, while we feel the guilt of doing so. Another back-and-forth volley of pity and regret. However, there comes this time when we know that pretending is going nowhere. Backed in a corner, it may be the first moment of honesty in a long time.

There is some relief. Maybe it could be good. But the fear of what comes next seems overwhelming once again. I admitted it had become "maybe a bit of a problem." Maybe I could find a way to make everyone happy, stop drinking when I need to see them, but still avoid quitting altogether. My dad was open to talking about it but said maybe he wasn't the best one to talk to about this. Perhaps it would be easier with someone else. My dad was one that did what many claims cannot be; he quit on his own. There were no meetings, no rehab, and no programs. One day, he decided he didn't want to be "the drunk guy" and never drank again. I would find out later there was more to it than that, but from all appearances, that is what happened. He also told me that he thought about what people would be saying at his funeral if he never quit. Perhaps they would say, "He was a good person; but too bad he was a drunk". That thought hit him hard as I could imagine. Of course, the fact that I held onto the idea that I could do the same and quit on my own for years did not bode well. He suggested I speak to a friend who had also quit drinking. My Dad stopping influenced him, but he, on the other hand quit drinking by frequenting the rooms of Alcoholics Anonymous. He embraced their philosophy, principles, and way of living to achieve a successful, productive, content, humble life without drinking or using.

Isn't that swell? What a bunch of Crap, huh? Well, it sounds good on paper, but not for me. I don't need that gathering with randos whining and complaining about their bad life. Remember, they are just a bunch of Losers, Slackers, and Amateurs. Given, my dad's buddy was a successful business owner with a good family, he was responsible, respectable, and happy, and people seemed to like him, but he must be the exception, right?

I am exaggerating my displeasure with this suggestion. When my dad asked me to meet with him, I wasn't that vehemently opposed and didn't say anything against AA. I didn't know much about it. I realized I needed a change but didn't want to quit. But, I needed some change. So, I was at least curious. I did meet with him. As I mentioned before, I had to have a few pops to "calm the nerves" over this situation, of course I did.

Here is the part where we have been called out. We do have a realization there is a problem. Loved ones have hope this will be a turning point. We must show or pretend we are doing something to appease everyone. But we still don't want to quit. How can we do better, not be so obvious and manipulate this situation, so everyone wins? They worry less, we do a little better, but still get to drink or use. We, addicts, are great (at least we think) at manipulating people and situations to get what we want.

Here began my introduction to the world of Recovery, of AA, of pretending to quit, of short periods of not drinking, of relapses of lots of denials, of appeasing, of start, stop, start to stop, followed by starting again, and rehab and detox and all forms of "research" to more relapse to different types of recovery groups on this crazy path to Sobriety. It sticks for some right away, not for me. There are many reasons for this; ego being a big one. You don't have to follow the path I took. It would be much easier for you and everyone you know. I was too stubborn and always thought I knew a better way.

My dad's friend went to AA. He did what they said to do, kept doing it, and did not go through all I did to get here. We all make our choices and earn prizes for them. He did plant a seed, though, which is important. He somehow got me to agree to wake up at 5 o'clock in the freaking morning every day for quite a stretch to go to these meetings. Sometimes, I had not slept well at all. Sometimes, I would sneak some "medicine" to feel better before going. But I went. To my surprise, these people were mainly relatively ordinary. Except that they got up at the crack of dawn, drove to this place, acted as they liked it, and often seemed cheerful doing it. WTF. This "lunacy" was the last thing I wanted to do.

Note that as one gains knowledge, our opinions of things change drastically. I will expound on this change later. At this point, however, this was just another necessary exercise to call off the hounds and get me back to doing what I wanted. I would attend these meetings and listen to all the stories of where these people came from, the depths they had recovered from, and the losses they endured. Compelling stories for certain. Admirable turnaround for sure. Nothing I would ever experience, of course, I thought. Some were still struggling with many things but were happy to be there. On the other hand, I still thought I was different in my superior mind. At first, I just listened and was welcomed there, as are most. People were kind. However, when I finally got to sharing, I would often spew justifications and minimize how much of a problem I had and how I didn't experience many things they were discussing. I would be witty and clever, bloviate about my education and all I have learned. I sometimes quoted things from outside AA to show how much I knew. I was not getting the real reason for this sharing experience. I was going to show them that I had this figured out and that I was just there to be a good example, not because I needed help. People listened knowingly in pity because they've seen countless people like me come in and out of AA thinking they know it all, but where it counted here, not knowing anything conducive to Recovery at all.

One time I went to a meeting at a place that was known as a low-point indigent detox place. I went there with my brother-in-law, who had been sober for many years, and AA helped him. This place was Non-Profit and Free to those that went there. Anyone could go there; the only stipulation is being loaded and needing a detox. There was no medical staff, but they had punch with lots of sugar to help prevent seizures from alcohol withdrawal, and there was a hospital nearby. Seizures were still a common occurrence here. In this place, the people waiting to get a bed there will sit, stay on couches, and even sleep there for more than a day, if necessary, waiting for someone else to leave. We went there with my brother-in-law's sponsor. A sponsor is an accountability partner or coach or someone who has been there and has gained some wisdom to share with others to help them find a solution. Of course, I was just there to observe and support my brother-in-law, not because I had a problem. No, not me!

I sat in this meeting looking at these people on the couches, shaking and sweating, trying to listen, but as I could ascertain, they wanted to be anywhere but there. They were dying for a drink, or They were just desperate to get checked in there, to sleep in a bed and have some miracle relieve them of the hell they were feeling right then. Most had this distant, desperate, hopeless look on their faces. Even though I had had my struggles, I recall looking at them and thinking, damn, good thing I will never be in a place like this, feeling or looking like these people right here. I couldn't imagine being in that place. Look out for what you can't imagine when it comes to addiction. Here was yet another - I WILL NEVER proclamation that may have been a prophecy. I sat on those very couches as a Non-Smoker chain, smoking cigarettes and waiting for a bed during Thanksgiving time, shaking from withdrawal after another bender about a year later. I can imagine the thoughts of some of the people that came to the evening meeting there, looking at me, shaking and baking, thinking - I WILL NEVER. That was another of the seven detox visits I incurred.

Another time I had agreed to go into a 30-day outpatient program. I would stay at home but go there from 9 am to 3:30 every day. They would do a pee test every morning. We would attend meetings, and therapy sessions, Meditate, smoke cigarettes on breaks, and do other activities. Then we would go home. Note: I have never been a smoker. I hate them. They smell horrible. However, I would become a chain smoker whenever I was in detox or trying to quit drinking. I thought it helped. Then after a period, they would make me sick again, and I would get sober for a while and stop that. Anyway, back in the program, I figured out that I could leave there, sit somewhere and drink and smoke cigarettes for about an hour or two, go home, buzz out for a while, eat, drink a lot of water, go to sleep, and pass the pee test in the morning if I had stopped at the right time. I did this almost every day I was in that program. I got caught once and had a little talking to. It was cough medicine for a cold, I said. I Had it all figured out. I got my Chip for completion of the program and got many congratulations and "we're proud of you" comments from my family. It was like a vacation, except for having to get up and drive to that place every morning to play the charade again with all the lovely counselors trying to help me. Congratulations, you fooled everyone again, got the heat off for a while, and didn't recover from anything. Yay. After I celebrated getting out of detox or a program for a time, I usually would realize I had to try and quit again, so I would attend meetings to attempt to make this stick again.

Why wasn't this AA thing working? It's broken. I've done rehab, and I've gone to tons of meetings. I had a sponsor. I was "Reading the Steps." Writing down many experiences, regrets, grievances, guilt, shame, and shit. Who harmed me, and who I may have hurt. Who I should make amends to, who I should forgive. It doesn't work. That's what we think, right? I am unsure if it had to do with not counting weekends, holidays, or special occasions, the drinking between meetings, or celebrating after getting 30, 60, or 90 days dry. That may have contributed, I suppose. They said it wasn't about perfection! They say it is about Progress. A lot of other people are making progress, certainly more than me. Why? Is it that obvious?

Cliché Alert: There is a Universal truth regarding anything worth anything you want to progress in and succeed. Whatever it is-

IT WILL ONLY WORK IF YOU WORK IT.

Anything that comes with great reward takes hard work or at least consistent, serious effort, the ability to listen, learn and be teachable. As much as we don't want it that way, things only happen with action; and sometimes it isn't easy. One must also be humble and realize that you are not God and don't know everything. Some with far less education can teach you more than you would ever believe. Age, gender, race, origin, or nationality doesn't matter. You can learn things you don't know. Often, they can teach you more of actual worth than you could ever teach them. Also, again this is not an advertisement for Religion. I do not consider myself very "religious." I do, however, believe in developing a relationship with something greater than myself. I call this God, and I do absolutely believe in Jesus as do many, but there is no mandate on what you name it as far as recovery goes. However, it is a necessity. Even if you are an atheist, I promise you, there is something greater than you. I don't care how smart we think we are. Look at this world. Look at the good and evil all around us. Look at nature. Look at all the goodness, kindness, amazing people, accomplishments, amazing places, animals, and things in the world. Look at all the danger, evil, pain, and suffering. Some of it we can explain. In some of it, there is no human explanation available. Unless we have dominion over all of this and have answers and solutions for all the bad things in the world, there is a higher power than us. Unless we are the only ones with love, wonder, and gratitude for all the good things in the world, there is a greater power. There are people wiser than us who have been there, tried all the nonsense, failed, changed their hearts and minds, and came out victorious. Unless we have recovered and the obsession and burden of addiction are in our past, we don't know everything, and there is something we can learn from someone and something more significant than us in this universe. Millions of people reach that goal, and so can we if we give up the idea that we can keep doing what we are doing and achieve anything but failure, insanity, or death. That's the hard Truth. We often know this in our hearts and mind but fail to do anything about it with our actions.

I could list many wild, crazy stories of all the false starts, the failures, health scares, and every detox or rehab visit. I could tell of close calls while driving drunk where I should have gotten caught or worse. But I was good at it! Oh, Boy, famous words. There are even a few miracles that make it possible for me to be here writing this right now. I have plenty of old fun, exciting, wild, and crazy memorable experiences from drinking too. There is no sense in denying or forgetting that. But we must live in the present. We must move forward from what was once good and has now turned sour. If you are like me, I am sorry to be the bearer of bad news or remind you of the Truth. The fun times of drinking and using are over. Trying to relive the past is a futile endeavor. To repeat the cliche - The past is a great place to learn from, not a great place to Live In.

Thus, I want to move on from the past and the pain to the solution. Don't be afraid, don't despair. I promise you there is good news. All we must do is change everything. Oh, damn, there I go painting an ominous, scary picture. No, the journey is good, fruitful, and rewarding. All you must do is believe you can do it and follow some difficult but simple steps if that makes sense. It will. Look at only part of the mountains we must climb. Just look at the first step. Do it right now. Stand up or roll forward or crawl a foot from wherever you are. How did that go? You did it. That is Progress. Did you trip or stumble a little? That is

Progress, not perfection. Now that we know we can accomplish something, we can achieve many things. I took years of denial, struggle, relapses, failures, and, more importantly, getting back up. The latter is the most important thing. The most important thing I ever did in my journey of Recovery is never to give up. As embarrassing as it is to admit mistakes, failure, and starting over, the one thing that stuck in my mind and carried me to today is "KEEP COMING BACK and DO NOT GIVE UP. "Just don't give up or give in. It is worth it. You are worth it.

Cliche alert : They say, "Build it, and they will come." It's true. Build your defenses, build your humbleness, build your confidence, build your strength, build your courage, build up your self-image, build your honesty, build your forgiveness, build your faith, and amazing things will come.

"Do Not Give up before the Miracle comes." It will if you let it.

EXPERIENCE YOUR OWN MIRACLE
ON THE TRANSFORMATIVE JOURNEY
FROM ALCOHOLISM AND ADDICTION
TO CONTENTMENT AND PEACE

"The only person you are destined to become is the person you decide to be."

— RALPH WALDO EMERSON PHILOSOPHER,
POET, AUTHOR, ESSAYIST

Earlier in this book, I mentioned that even when human beings don't know each other, they can have a deep awareness of where someone else has been, what they have felt, and the causes of their pain.

As someone who has been through the journey of alcohol addiction recovery, I know that even a person in the throes of deep denial can grow in peacefulness, sobriety, and contentment. My aim in this book is to share the strategies that helped and the things I know are true.

We are all different, yet in some ways, we are the same. We all have undeniable needs such as the need to be understood, heard, and loved. We may have led vastly different lives, been through unique experiences, and harbored our own set of beliefs, but more things unite than divide us.

As you embark on your own voyage of self-discovery, you may have come across other people who are seeking freedom from addiction. Like you, they may be reaching for the light at the end of the tunnel. They may know, deep within their hearts, that miracles can, and do happen.

If you know someone who is burdened by guilt because they have hurt loved ones or lost out on life opportunities because of addiction, you can be the voice that lets them know that they can experience profound change and healing.

They may be struggling to find a sense of purpose and peace. However, they will not experience contentment and joy until they stop blaming or punishing themselves, and start acknowledging the choices they made. You know how hard this balance can be to strike, but you also know that it is necessary if you are seeking a better future.

You have also discovered that the process of recovery is made infinitely more bearable when we have support. If my book has helped you discover how to set your big goal and stick to it with perseverance, you may want to share the knowledge you have gained with other readers. In doing so, you can empower them to discover that self-forgiveness takes work, humbleness, and—for many people—a connection to a greater power than ourselves.

By leaving a review of this book on Amazon, you'll help other people find peace, sobriety, and happiness once again.

Simply by telling them how this book helped you and what they can expect to find inside, you'll help them understand that a sober, content, productive life is possible if you truly want and seek it. Sober living miracles happen every day!

Please leave a brief, honest review when you complete the book or even right now. It would mean a lot and will spread the message of hope.

5

HOLY SHITE ON A KITE

I AM ONE OF THOSE PEOPLE

D enial is exhausting. But it is what we do.

Once we get over that and start telling the truth, we may have a chance.

Once the "switch has flipped for us," the fun is gone, and the vicious cycle has taken hold; it is a pointless exercise to keep lying (not that lying is ever good). By the way, everyone but us already knows the truth. It is an insult to the intelligence and strain on the patience, perseverance, and understanding of everyone in our lives to keep pretending that we aren't struggling for our lives. That is the reality, and once we are addicted, it truly is life or death.

We can one day realize how absurd all the things we will do, and how hard we fight the obvious, when we can see it from a more transparent, longer view. It's not unlike how the drunken conversations, jokes, comments, ideas, revelations, and philosophizing may sound so clever, funny, deep, mind-blowing, and profound to the ears of us totally loaded people in our full glory. However, when witnessed as a sober person just sounds ridiculous, sometimes annoying, belligerent, stupid, chemically retarded, and relatively pitiful. If we only knew, we sounded like that. We do, or I mean other drunks do. Not me, of course. Ha!

Yet, we keep on with this denial, thinking it somehow preserves any remnant of dignity and control over our lives. It just perpetuates the opposite. It is digging a deeper hole and adding to the wreckage, regrets, loss, and disappointments strewn across our lives. The more we pile up, the harder it will be for those that care for us even to see us. Seeing what Hope looks like over the wreckage will be more challenging. It seems so overwhelming at times. There is still Hope!

No matter who one is or what recovery program we go through or don't, where we come from, or how bad things have gotten, there are conditions even to have this Hope. To realize any goals in our lives, to see the potential we once believed in, to elevate our self-image, and to recover from addiction, there exist many things that MUST occur to stop this cycle and stay sober. Even my dad, who "quit on his own" after years of heavy drinking, had to follow certain things to realize the miracle. There is no point in sugarcoating it. There is no point in leaving a cliffhanger for the end of the book so that you keep on reading. It would be negligent and pointless not to tell you such essential requisites that I know to be true right now. Without them, progress is tenuous at best.

The point of this book is to share experience, strength, Hope, and even share failure and success and to encourage the belief in the possibility of a sober, content, productive, contributing, fruitful, happy, and joyful life for those who want it and seek it. You may know some of the prerequisites to achieve this goal, and we will get to the things that help us through, but we must understand the non-negotiable necessities to make it happen.

Some will struggle for years focusing on the wrong things, doing the same things, and achieving nothing. You don't want to do that and don't have to.

I did do that for years. It was a fruitless battle, besides the lessons, I now may share. So, none of our experiences or struggles are useless after all. I learned from the past, and I don't live in it.

Therein lies one of the keys. It is for those who want it, really WANT it.

I went for years running in circles while deep in my heart, for much of that time, I didn't want it. Not enough to make it happen anyway. You Must WANT it as if your life depends on it. Your life does depend on it. Understand, this does not mean you want it only because others want it for you, because others are forcing you or the law demands you. You must want it wholeheartedly- for yourself. It is not enough if you only do it because others want you to, even though you love them. You must want it for yourself. Now, this may seem self-serving. You may think - Here we are, the ones causing all this hurt. Aren't people already thinking and telling us we are selfish, and you say I am only to do this for myself? Not exactly. But - at the core, yes. It must be for you.

Newsflash -- Recovery is full of confounding conundrums, which may sound counterintuitive. Keep an open mind. Carry on.

It is imperative that if we have loved ones that we care about, we do consider their feelings; we want to have them stop worrying about us. It matters that we care about what our actions do to them. It matters that we are not inconsiderate of others. It matters not to be an insensitive prick. Nobody likes or wants to be around an insensitive prick. But that's not us. If it is, we can even change that, and you should.

That all matters. It still must be because YOU want it for YOU. Others will surely reap benefits as well. We still must do it because we want it, or it won't happen. If we can't love ourselves enough to change, it will be hard for anyone else to love us enough to stay. It is too painful. Likely, if you are like most addicts, in your mind, you never stop caring for those that love you. You are devastated that they hurt. Still, you keep doing what you are doing. Right? "I don't do the good things I want to do, and I keep doing the evil things I don't want to do." WE must want it for us for anyone to get it, and that is the reality.

But wait, there's more! Not only do we have to want it, but we also must Believe we can have it. Many want it and never get it because they never truly believe they can have it. Believing in anything first is essential to having the will to obtain it. It may seem like common sense to some. It is not as commonly understood as we may think. The self-image dramatically influences our perception of ourselves and may be so damaged that we can no longer see our dreams, goals, and potential. Some believe this is their fate, to suffer and die burdened and beholden to addiction. They think they never were or can never again be worthy or capable of living without servitude to this affliction, pain, and suffering. So, sadly, that is what many addicts get. It may be a distant glimmer, but they do not comprehend how or have any foreseeable path to manifest this "Good Life" out there in the way far distance. It is too overwhelming, and they fixate on the impossibility of reaching the destination without seeing that the first step is right there. That is all we must be concerned with now. That one first step leads to possibility. Possibility leads to Hope; Hope leads to action; action leads to progress, and progress gives us broken, eternally imperfect people a chance.

I experienced a sad example of this firsthand one time. It was when I had been sober for a stretch again. My wife and I happened upon a homeless young man. He was lying down on the sidewalk in a reasonably nice neighborhood, looking distressed. We stopped to see that he was ok. He had just become exhausted trying to walk up a hill to get where he was going. We gave him some water. We spoke a little and ended up giving him a ride. He told us his story of becoming estranged from his family and battling mental illness. He admitted he struggled with drugs too. When we dropped him off, I asked for his number and asked if we could meet for coffee sometime. I offered to take him to a meeting to check it out, and he agreed. I met him this one time; I bought him some shoes. I took him to this meeting. He sat through it. It was apparent he felt out of place. I met with him another time and offered to take him to our church group. I told him that he could get out of this, and I would help him. I told him we could be friends and I could introduce him to others. He cried at the thought that someone would even do this. The look I saw in his eyes was one of disbelief and appreciation. Yet, I think disbelief was the overlying thing in his mind. I called him again to take him to eat and go to this meeting. He never answered, and I never saw him again. It was sad. I don't think he believed this opportunity to change his life could be real. Not for him. I am sure he didn't want to stop using either. But the disbelief that this could happen assured that any of it wouldn't. Not at that point, anyway. I have prayed for that dude many times. He seemed like a good person.

I must admit. I learned another thing from this. Aside from wanting to help this person, I also wanted it to be ME, the one that could save this guy. There was some ego to that, as if I could be his savior and feel good and impressed with myself. I am far from that. I wanted to help; I was NOT his savior. I cannot make him, nor anyone else, make any changes they don't want. Neither can you. That is above our pay grade. We can offer to share our experience and present others an opportunity to aspire and believe they can change. That is all we can do. That is all anyone on this Earth can do for us as well. We must want it and have to believe it ourselves. Redundant but important.

I am here to tell you that the burden of addiction is not fate, written in blood and carved in stone for anyone if we follow specific steps to change our path. I don't even mean the actual

Twelve Steps about which we all hear. I don't negate them by any means, either. I will address those as well, for sure. Those steps are certainly blessings, and they are genuinely a map of miracles written and passed on from the wise that came before us. What I am talking about is related but even more fundamental in necessity than the invaluable map. It is first the desire and faith enough even to open the map. Then we will get to use the map.

The first requirements were wanting and the belief in possibility. When these elude us, we only believe in doing what we have always done while expecting a better result. We know what that is, and it is insanity. The game is over before you start. Not only that, but you also lack the quarter to play the game in the first place. You must want it and believe it is possible. It is possible; if you still think otherwise, it's just a lie from the enemy.

How many freaking awful stories have you heard about rock stars or other celebrities. The debauchery, the inconceivable quantities of alcohol and drugs abused at levels that should kill an elephant. Yet some of these freaks of rock and roll nature survive for years. Look at Keith Richards!!! Many perish, for sure. Sadly, so many. Some of them Survive! Against all odds, some survive and live to tell the tale, oft filled with horror. Then, even they may show redemption and recovery. Miracles! Their stories are like many others. At some point, however, they followed specific steps utterly contrary to what they ever conceived or believed they would ever do before and survived. They are wonders of the world! You can be one too!

The list continues.

You not only have to want it and believe you can get it, this Good Life of Sobriety, Contentment, and Joy, you have to decide to have it. You must decide to do something about it. You must make a decision that you are going to do what it takes to get there. You must make a choice. You will either do what you have been doing, wait forever, aimlessly for it to bring different results, and live in a world of despair, delusion, denial, and servitude to self-destruction. Or, you choose to change, believe, work for change, and know you can change, know it is good, is needed, and will give you Hope and possibility for this Good Life.

I realize that some will say we addicts don't have a choice. It is a disease, and we don't choose to do it. If we could choose, we wouldn't do it. We do it because we have no choice. OK. That is a hot steaming load of CRAP. That is a cop-out. It is easy to put off our bad decisions on someone or something else and not be held responsible. I am not belittling the power, persuasiveness, and torture of addiction. However, we always have a choice. We always make decisions. Usually, in active addiction, we make the wrong choice. It is still a choice. Every time I was in front of the liquor store after a stretch of sobriety as that obsession kicked in, and I debated my brain whether I should buy it and drink it or should I drive away and talk to someone immediately, two things could happen. I picked one, usually the wrong one. So, there was a choice. Every time I was lying in bed withdrawing and trying to fight the urge to "get well" by driving to the store or searching through the closet for more liquor, there were two things that could happen. I chose, usually, the wrong choice. The options are there. We usually pick the wrong one.

Now, we must start realizing that reality. There IS a choice. It is not an easy one to make in addiction. That is certain. However, we must want to make the right choice and believe and understand we can make the right choice. Someday we will get to where we KNOW we will make the right choice. It really can happen.

Oh, but we still need to finish the list.

Besides wanting and believing in the possibility, deciding about it, and making the right choice, one must also be willing to take action, work at it, and do things you do not necessarily want to do. We must be open to doing things that are contrary to usual, something we aren't used to, out of our comfort zone. Don't panic. It gets easier eventually. I promise. But there is no getting around it. You must do things differently. Making significant changes takes hard work. However, unless we talk metaphorically, it isn't like the "hard work" of digging ditches. There will be digging into how we got here and how to get out. Significant changes are necessary for survival in recovery. There is no getting around that. Significant changes from the inside out and all around are essential. The Good News is if you resolve to make them, you won't regret it. They will be challenging. That is certain, I guarantee; however, the rewards will be evident, invaluable, and irreplaceable, and you will be amazed, inspired, and grateful. It's waiting for you.

Another thing. You will hear much about a "Higher Power" in recovery. People have different thoughts about this. I have many ideas about this. I think recovery should be possible, available, not judgmental, not exclusive to any "Religion," and there for anyone who needs it, which is anyone who is addicted to alcohol or drugs. Alcoholics Anonymous did have its beginnings, influenced by Religious Principles back when they would send alcoholics or drug addicts to insane asylums because they didn't know what to do with them or how to heal them or their insanity.

When Bill Wilson brought AA equally to the secular masses and agnostics, not only religious, bringing alcoholics together in fellowship to share their experiences, strength, and Hope, an amazing thing happened. These people began to recover. The fact that it is very inclusive to all who need them does not take away from the fact that the "Higher Power" theory is a core principle of the program. The book and the program refer to God a lot. Often people do develop a relationship with what they call God. But there is undoubtedly no forcing of religion in AA. That's why it will say God as you understand it to be. I know what God means to me. However, there is no mandate on what that means to each person.

While I consider my "higher power" God and have my own beliefs for many good observable reasons, and many other people do as well, this in no way excludes those with different views or that don't believe in God. I would not wish anything to hold anyone back on a journey to recovery, and your recovery is your recovery. It is amazing what happens to our views when incredible things begin to happen, though. Things occur that we may not have thought possible. We may even begin to believe in miracles. Keep an open mind. With all this said, the principle of belief in a Power greater than us is not hard to imagine and is critical in this Journey. I mean, come on. In this vast, inconceivably massive Universe, the idea that we, the addict, and even "normal" humans, are the Highest Power around is improbable, would you not say? That may be one of the many very arrogant thoughts we think. We, who have made such a mess of much, are in control of everything and all-powerful? Is that a rational assumption? Then how did we get where we got? We have not even been able to control our lives, let alone the Universe or most of the things that happen in it. It would take more faith to believe that than it does to consider a "Higher Power" as a possibility. Fair? Bear with me. It will make sense, and you will see the purpose of this principle.

More succinctly, believing in a power greater than us, in whatever way that manifests for you, is also one of the requirements for recovery. I genuinely believe it; I have witnessed, felt, and lived it. It should give us peace that all the burdens are not only upon our shoulders to face alone, and they are not. There is a power greater than we alone that can help us fight these battles.

OK. Here is the last one before we open that map and see what's up and where we are going.

This one is crucial. It is hard. It will take patience and perseverance. We may need some rewiring. It may take a psychic reboot and a spiritual makeover. They are all crucial and challenging, but I want to emphasize this as it may have tripped me up, derailed my train, monkeyed with my wrench, sent me astray many times and prolonged my recovery journey as long as it did.

Ready? You can't drink or use! Does that seem too obvious? It is NOT obvious at all to most addicts. Even if we get some of the other requirements down, we always try to navigate around this one. We may have plans and justifications to "dabble" or "tone down" while investigating this recovery. Well, it won't work, not for a true alcoholic or addict. Once you flip the switch into addiction, no amount of dabbling leads to the "Good Life" I speak of. You either want it or you don't, and this is a deal breaker for what should be obvious reasons. We may get away with it temporarily and think we can walk the line between good intentions and half-measures, and it is usually short-lived.

I cannot count the times after a period of sobriety that I "dabbled" on some vacation far away and had a few beers. I got away with it. Nobody knew. Except, I knew. Even that is a kink in our armor. It is so common. A few months later, another opportunity will present itself, and we think the last time wasn't so terrible. I didn't go off the rails, and nobody knew. I can do the same this time—another Kink. Our honesty, integrity, and faithfulness to ourselves are in doubt now, and we add to our secrets. This time we have six drinks, and so on, until we drink every day and say, how did we get back here again? You will eventually learn about half-measures. They avail us nothing in the end.

It is not only not drinking or using. It is more, which is the hard part that scares people away because they look at it through the mind of an addict. We think, "you mean I have not to drink or use ever?" While this is true and seems so ominous at the time, it is imperative. It would be best if you didn't look at it as the doom of never drinking or using again. I want you to try and frame it differently and be open to the belief and possibility that you will one day say - I GET to NOT drink or use; what an effing relief, hallelujah, I am in Love with this. Seem improbable? Only if you don't want it or believe it.

You must give up the idea that someday if you take a break long enough, you can drink and not revert right back to where you were with all the consequences and the not very fun prizes.

I had so many "sobriety dates." I got on the revolving door of 30 days, 90 days, six months, and finally got a year. Then I went out, then a year again, then two years. Oooops. 2 years again. Over and over. If you know what newcomer and progress chips are, I had enough to melt down, build a boat and sail away. But I kept standing up and coming back, which is the only reason I am here.

I was getting the wanting-it part. I was doing steps, doing work, making progress and changes. However, as long I went, the more I learned with all the research, advice, growing faith, and significant changes -there was one thing that got me. I know this now. As much as I didn't want to admit it, even to myself, I always held on to the idea that I would be fine one day. If I wait long enough, I can enjoy the ole drink to "wind down" like "Normal" people again. Someday, you know, just a cocktail or glass of wine in the evening or cold ones on a summer day. Not now, but someday down the road, when I "graduate ," when I am "cured." I held onto that little thought in my mind for years. The only thing is that thought kept crawling forward and telling me - why wait? You feel good right now. This time it will be different. From repeated experience, ultimately, it is never different, leading to the same dead end.

I know forever seems like FREAKIN forever, but don't consider climbing the entire mountain at once. Just take the first step. Think of it as something other than forever, ten years, three months, or one week. Just think about today and what that next step is. Try to believe that one day you will be grateful to say - I will not be drunk or wasted today. I get not to put off life and responsibilities today. I get to be in control today. I get to be content today. I get to be at peace, and I get to look forward to tomorrow today.

One thing at a time. On task at a time. One goal at a time. One day at a time.

Want it. Believe you can have it.

Decide to get it.

Choose to take action.

Work for it.

Believe there is a Higher Power than us with more power than we alone to help conquer the battles we face.

Don't drink or use.

Give up the idea that you can drink or use without the eventual chaos, destruction, the same results, and proving insanity again.

You Really Can do this.

Let's explore how.

6

I WANT IT; I NEED IT; I HAVE TO HAVE IT; GIVE IT TO ME NOW!

One thing about the addict, alcoholics, and humans is that, in general, we want instant gratification in our fundamental nature. This desire did not happen only when we became addicts. When we were kids and hungry, we would scream our eyes out until we got what we needed. We usually would get what we wanted, if not only to stop us from crying for it. The more often we are immediately given what we want, the less tolerance and patience we have when we must wait for what we need. When parents don't let us learn about delayed gratification for what we want when kids, it becomes more ingrained that our desires will manifest immediately when older and becoming accustomed to instant gratification is detrimental to our peace and contentment. Now, in the world where you can get most things you need from an app on your phone, brought to your door, picking you up, or providing entertainment at your fingers, this addiction to instant gratification has become even worse. We see people in restaurants not talking to each other because they are glued to their phones to see how many likes their latest post got or, for FOMO, Fear of Missing Out on something. That addiction has made it so we are isolated even when sitting with a group of people. Do you notice how we panic if we step away anywhere, and we don't have our phones? I am still guilty of that. The phone is all-powerful, and it can feed our instant gratification with the lift of our wrist and the touch of a finger. People even deliver mind-altering substances and drugs to your door via an app or FedEx. Just what an addict needs, right?

The thing about instant gratification, it is trying to quench an aching need for something quickly. It also shoots us with a dopamine hit that gives us a rush, instant satisfaction, and excitement. The thing about it is that it is temporary. When the thrill wears out, we want to repeat that. This feeling does not only apply to addicts, nor only pertains to alcohol or drugs. It could be anything that gives us a rush or some satisfaction. It could even be exercise if we were doing a healthy thing. It can also be entertainment, food, sex, getting likes on social media, or even buying things. We can get addicted to the rush of any of those things. The problem with this rush is that it is temporary. It doesn't last.

Have you ever gotten so excited to buy something, and by the time you get it, some of the rush has already worn out, and a week later, you hardly care that you have it? It can be more about the wanting than it is about the having. Not with drugs and alcohol; we scarf those up right away. But, as you may notice, sometimes the anticipation, once you know you will get high or drunk, is almost as much of a rush as getting loaded. Once you have what you need, getting loaded calms you down from that anticipation and exhilaration. Once again, though, the feeling is temporary. With substance abuse and addiction, you must repeat this cycle again and again to maintain. Your tolerance rises, so you also must do more and more.

Of course, we seek this rush again over and over because we like it. Eventually, we seek it because we need it. What we are doing, though, is running from other things. Often, seeking this rush can be solely about trying to distract us from other things: feelings of shyness, lack of confidence, low self-image, inadequacy, regrets, resentments, shame, guilt, pain, and trauma. It is these things where the origin of our real problems lies. Alcohol and drugs or any other thing we are addicted to are just what we run to in avoiding our real issues. They do, however, become a problem themselves, leading to us checking out, neglecting responsibilities, and relationships, running from life, and never facing the feelings or issues that drove us to numb ourselves with substances in the first place. Or, eventually, anyway.

So, when we have been running on instant gratification seeking for years and years, we finally come to the point where we have at least admitted we have to try to make a change, for one reason or another. Do you think the addiction to instant gratification will suddenly disappear when it comes to seeking Recovery? Not a chance. When we come to a moment where we are willing to try it, we still want it to work right now! Because we have things to do, people to see, and places to go, right? This is why we say when trying to encourage someone into Recovery that there are only fleeting moments when we are willing, and that is when we must act on it.

How much patience do you think one will initially have when considering being "cured"? Not a hell of a lot, I will tell you that right now. So, getting clean or putting down the bottle is just one of the things we must get over. Many of the other things are even more complex, and often not assimilating to the other changes is what drives us back to the drug of choice once again. We have no patience. Patience is another thing required for Recovery. Patience, perseverance, and replacing habits ingrained for years with new ones that will improve our lives instead of destroying them are fundamental and essential.

We must get used to delayed gratification. The things we learn and do will give us fulfilling, solid, and more lasting satisfaction, contentment, and joy, guaranteed if we resolve to and commit to these steps. Most worthwhile things come from steady work over time than from quick fixes. The problem is we want it now. Now, now, now!

Once, before I ever really got into any authentic, committed recovery, my wife and I started going to a local Church. I thought maybe that would give me inspiration. It couldn't hurt, right? It didn't hurt. It helped in many ways, Not to stop drinking, though. I thought, eventually, it would. IT would make ME stop. I didn't know much about Recovery at that time. I even thought that perhaps if I got Baptized, that would make me stop. When the Pastor we had just met plunged me under that water, I pictured all desire to do wrong or to drink too much would wash away, and I could be "normal" again. It was quite a request to make under the circumstances. Man, I was so loaded when he plunged me into that water. I was looking forward to that day being "cured." I had a hangover, and I just couldn't keep myself from "getting well" to feel better while doing it. I did not sober up or quit when I came out of the water. That is not how it works and there is more for us to do. My sponsor at the time was there. He knew I was drunk and was not ready to stop. I later spoke to the Pastor about it. He understood, he could smell it. Everyone knew it. They even have it on video after 15 years at that Church. Classic. This was not one of the proudest moments for me. Yikes.

He wouldn't deprive me of wanting to be baptized just because I was drunk. The only hope was that I did mean what I said was committing to that day, confessing my faith, and committing to "leave the old ways behind." Faith had grown, leaving the old ways , not quite. Um, yeah, I had to do that all over again several years later. I just wanted to have addiction washed away that day. I was not stating I was ready to commit myself to being sober and more like Jesus. I did believe in God. I just thought that was how he worked, and he would do me a solid by curing me immediately, like right there. It does not work that way. We must learn patience and delayed gratification. We desperately must.

We have been running and gunning for so long; if it is not evident that it will take time to change our ways, I am not sure what could make it so obvious. But it still takes a literal act of God to ingrain the idea of patience, slow and easy, one day at a time, into our demanding brain.

When we first get into recovery mode, which takes a long time in the scheme of our story, many of the things we hear seem like slogans and sad stories. Many people have been going through it for a very long time and have seen people like us come and go and disappear daily. What is the difference between them and us? Well, we don't know anything about all of this or how it works, don't believe it, and think we know better than everyone about everything. They have wisdom, have seen and made it work, are still alive, and are still sitting in the same place every day. They may not even feel they have to do meetings anymore, but they choose to, in part to see it work again for arrogant, green, know-all people like us, even though they know it won't work for more than it will. This is not because the program doesn't work; but, only because most don't commit to recovery or work the program as it is recommended and illustrated by those for whom it is working. A million others will come and go and never return. They don't want it, don't believe it can happen and are not willing to decide to work for it. IT being a good, humble, content, happy, productive life full of joy and less drama without numbing ourselves to reality. I was undoubtedly one of those. But for some reason, I kept getting up and coming back.

How do we make it work for us now that we have a moment of willingness? Besides all the necessary and non-negotiable prerequisites, I mentioned in the last chapter, many things will help. Be clear: None of these alone will be an instant cure for all that ails us. We embark on a process, an overhaul, and each good thing we do for ourselves will contribute to positive changes that build upon each other. None of them gives us a pass to "graduate early." This game has no graduation, but for the day, we die happy and are not loaded. That's graduation. But the good thing is if we do many of these things, graduation is a long, long time away, it's eternal, and we get to enjoy the journey along the way.

Set a big goal, forget about it, and focus on the one step before you. Once you set the goal, obsessing over the destination only distracts you from the only thing you can really achieve, which is what is in front of you right now.

Have you ever heard the idea that if you focus on everything all at once, you will do nothing well and will likely fail? It's true.

You set a big goal, so you have a target. It may seem far away, but at least it is real. You know where you are going, and you and you believe you can get there. This takes a lot of faith. You may not be used to achieving anything big or small at any time recently. Or you are used to attaining everything too quickly. Either way, there is a reason we are here, so we know there is something we want at the end of this desire, wish, or prayer. If all we can manage is imagining a target in the distance, believe there is a path that someone knows. When you get there, there will be rewards. That's it. Now forget it. Now focus on taking one step, one thing that is good for you today.

To illustrate this, think of a professional mountain climber. Imagine the mountain of things we must figure out or fix. Now back to the mountain climber. When the mountain climber sets out to tackle a large mountain, he aims to get to the top of it. However, he doesn't start compiling pictures of the summit or talk about what he will do when he arrives there or how he will jump up and down at the top like Rocky Balboa. He doesn't think about what he will have for breakfast the next day or how many people will tell him how awesome he is for making it to the top. No. He first looks at a map. He figures out the best place to start. He talks to people about the approach. He goes to the location. He investigates the weather. He figures out what equipment he will need. He starts walking, then maybe running to build up his stamina. He exercises to get fit. He eats well to be well-nourished and healthy. He does exercises for his lungs to handle the altitude. He does many other things one at a time. He feels strong, confident, and ready. Then, he steps foot at the location. He rechecks everything and then takes the first step. There is no need to think about the top of that mountain. He better sure pay attention to every step along the way in front of him, however.

Don't think you are going to solve all your problems and clean up all your messes right away. To even think of reaching a goal, we must focus on taking one step, doing the next good thing, and not drinking or using just for today.

Cliche alert: You may get tired of it. However, in our position and for anyone, it makes sense and makes the task before us more conceivable. It's One day at a time, and that's the only way you get to the next one.

Once I started at least listening to others more than trying to prove how smart I was, I began to not only be able to make real progress but be able to identify those that, just like me, thought we could cure ourselves upon command with only our knowledge, intellect, and self-will. It is a sad ability because we know where it usually ends up. Because I at least came back even when I fell, I witnessed many come in with enthusiasm, motivation, and ready to get a grip, take control, impress everyone, and be the Boss of Recovery! Only this self-willed rush of adrenaline and resolve to knock out this recovery thing at record speed and get to rule the world loses its shiny gloss over a bit of time. Reality reveals itself, and finding they can't tackle this like they tackled the prom court, dodgeball at school, or witty banter at the water cooler at work, they lose interest, lose control again, and do not come back.

Believe in the summit. Don't try to run there in record time; you might end up as a landmark or frozen hump before you are halfway up.

Have an open mind, do one good thing, one first step. Listen to those that have been there instead of speaking at first. Don't drink or use, and that's a good beginning.

I am describing a scene as if we are already attending recovery meetings. If I can speak from experience and based on the path of millions of success stories before me, that is where we should be, especially in early Recovery. Then we will talk about where we should be in the future. Let's think about today. There are countless reasons why we should be there, not the least of which is to be around like blinded people. Be where there are people who know what it's like, people who have been there, people who have done ALL of that, people who tried and failed and came back, people have come and stayed and never left, people who have wisdom and people who understand what we are going through, don't judge you, want you to win and are willing to put up with you. It's a good place. Like anything involving people, there will be places that don't click for you, with people you can't relate to. Things will be said that don't hit home. Pick the things

that do and the people you relate to, or at least the ones that are willing to invest in your recovery. There is a place for you with good people as broken as you and those that have your back. There are meetings all over every city. Don't be over-selective. Humble yourself. Don't be arrogant and judgmental. Find the place. Don't overthink it.

We can do countless practical things that will help in our Recovery. We can do many things related to our health and well-being outside of recovery meetings that will be essential in our journey to a happy, humble, healthy, content, joyful sober life. All of that is just as important as we must live in the real world again eventually. However, creating a foundation to build this new "Good Life" to withstand time, turmoil, real life, and ups and downs is also essential. Recovery meetings are a good start. Some good people will help and share this journey with us; you might even make some life-long, authentic friends.

My recovery journey began when I was convinced and coerced to attend AA. Though I took a path of most resistance, choosing just the parts I wanted, leaving out the rest, riding the revolving door, and just not getting it at first, it was still invaluable; it planted seeds for the future and improved my life and wisdom immeasurably. It is still a big part of why I am here, even though I have also experienced different types of recovery groups, fellowship groups, gatherings, and many with valuable resources with different people. They have all been invaluable in one way or the other.

Our propensity to want things now is not common only to addicts and alcoholics as we can quickly establish watching human nature. People go through diet after diet, looking for the one that will magically work with the least effort or sacrifice. People take supplements that promise to help them lose weight "without diet or exercise." People buy gadgets that are going to "Rub off the Fat." The Eat Cake Lose Weight diet would be a blockbuster hit! People buy hundreds of millions of dollars each year in exercise equipment, hoping to get that machine that will do all the hard work for them. This time I am going to stick with it! Every January, gyms are full, and Amazon is pumping out more and more health and fitness Miracles to all those out there who will finally get fit and stay healthy. By February, the gyms are back to the regulars, the resolutions are forgotten, the machine is a clothes hangar, and the recliner feels very comfy. Maybe next year. We want the quickest result with the least effort for everything. In Recovery, as with health and fitness, slow and steady, realistic, and consistent will build foundations of lasting results. However, with Recovery from addiction in many cases, there is no "maybe next year." Some ride this roller coaster year after year; some don't get to see next year at all, sadly.

Taking things slow and steady and setting realistic goals and expectations are essential in general health and Recovery. We often stop drinking or using for some time when we finally commit to Recovery. We start sleeping, eating, and feeling stronger and healthier, and we like it. It is an exciting feeling, and we feel like we are back! We feel like we've got this now. Graduation is near! Some will call this the "Pink Cloud" phenomenon. Beware!

It feels good. We may feel accomplished. One may undoubtedly feel excited and much more energized. There is nothing wrong with feeling more enthused and motivated and thinking clearer after maybe years of feeling numb, clouded, lethargic, and perhaps even hopeless.

We may feel like a new person already. We must not get cocky, and feel like we have accomplished Recovery because we feel better now. This can be a vulnerable time and one in which many relapses occur. The first 90 days can bring a sense of overconfidence followed by a letdown when you can't maintain this enthusiasm and excitement and when we must again deal with the circumstances of real life. Recovery is like emotions, energy, and life itself, full of ups and downs, highs and lows. What we are aiming for is steady. When we can get to a place where the highs are not extreme, and the lows are not severe, and we can better handle emotions and circumstances, remaining calm and addressing things as they come without being overwhelmed or too excited, we have made significant progress. This will take time, and we must be aware of that. Whenever we feel we have it all figured out, we're cured and no longer need help, we must stop ourselves, close our eyes, take a deep breath, and remember this is for the rest of our lives, not just a sprint. Start over, go back to the basics, and humble your-self. Instant gratification is what we need to get over.

I realize everyone's circumstance is different. For everyone, though, Recovery must become our priority. I know we will say, what about my family? What about my job? I must get back in the game. I want to make everything up to everyone right away. I need to hustle and get ahead. I don't want to think about this stuff anymore. I just want to be normal and get back to my life. Trust me; I was there. I thought (first mistake) that "Getting back to life" as fast as possible would make me feel better, feel accomplished, make people not think I was an F-Up, and prove I had it all under control now. That's all great, and we will get there. But if we "jump back into life" as if we never had a problem, we would do the same thing we had done before, looking for a quick fix. We will try to stuff all this past we had in a box, leave it behind, and never really address any of the things that got us here in the first place, and relapse and return to insanity are almost inevitable with the quick-fix approach.

This was my method of operation from the start. My initial thought was always, "well, my dad did it on his own; I can do the same thing. I am smart. I have willpower." I've never used willpower, but I have it. I must make up my mind and use it. Well, basing our Recovery and how we approach it on another person's circumstance is a recipe for failure. Everyone is different. I am not saying it hasn't been done. Let's not base our life and survival on "yeah, but this guy did it." It can happen, but it doesn't mean it is something that will last. Keeping this a priority and following specific proven steps will make for a more lasting, less painful, less suffering way to reach our goal of a happy, healthy, content, joyful sober life. As I stated in the beginning, even though my dad was reasonably independent in his Recovery, he did have help from others; he did have to suffer difficulty, did have to learn a lot, and did have to maintain a lot of boundaries. He had to follow requirements to remain sober as long as he did. I made more progress when I stopped using his journey as my path.

Now, we addicts always want to cause trouble and point out ways to question, protest and prove other people wrong or say we contradict ourselves so we can feel superior.

We usually do want to feel superior. Thus, you may say, Hey, but you say not to base your Recovery on another person's, yet you are telling us to follow all of this stuff just because you did and others did. Isn't that being sheep? It is not. Yes, I share my experience and what I have learned through trial and error, failure, and success. I am not a doctor, scientist, or Prophet. I am just a person who has been through what many others have, and I have also learned many things that millions of people over decades and decades have also experienced similarly. Often, we were arrogant and questioned everything all along the way. We also wondered why we couldn't stay sober, trying it our way or that one guy's way while others were sober for years and decades. Is aspiring to replicate success being sheep? OK, Baaaa. I will never say that everyone's Recovery will look the same. Mine is certainly not like everyone else's. I know the things that work for me and am sharing them. If that One Guy has a different way that works and wants to write a book about this One Guy's Method to Stay Sober and Rule the world- he is free to do it. I will celebrate anyone's success. It is never to say that everything that I or anyone else says is gospel and must be followed by the letter. That would be another return to arrogance, self-importance, and above my pay grade. We take what works for us and has worked for many and stick to it. Just make sure one's mind is open, and we are willing to accept that we don't know everything, others know more than us, and there is a power greater than us humans.

Whatever we do, there is no question that Recovery must be a priority in our lives. Without it, all else will crumble. Suppose we have gotten to this place where addiction has taken over our lives. In that case, the only way to get it back is to replace it with the things that will help us manage our lives, our relation-ships, our jobs, our attention to our kids, and our productivity and achieve this healthy, happy, productive, content sober life we aim for. We have proved over and again that we cannot manage all these things and keep them if we are drinking and using and having this addiction and obsession take priority over all the things we claim to care about. It must be number one. It is the foundation from this day forward. Even if this sounds overbearing and not fun and like destiny towards a captive boring life, I assure you that that is not the case. Were we not captive and in bondage before? Is it enjoyable when all we can do is think about, seek, and do whatever is necessary for that next drink or fix? Of course, it wasn't. Life is going to be so much better. It will get more manageable and rewarding, and you will love it, my promise. But you must want, believe, and work at it. These changes will not make life all candy, roses, and free money. Life is life. Life Is hard. However, we will be able to handle anything that comes our way by leaps and bounds so much better than when we are numb to it all, oblivious and incapable as we were when we were loaded. This is something I can tell you from intimate personal experience, and I promise it's true.

It is incredible how life works sometimes and how timing works. Thank God I got sober, and it finally stuck when it did. I went through a lot during my journey going back and forth in Recovery, and my wife and I went through a lot. However, I had not experienced much loss of loved ones that were close to me. Except when I was 27, I witnessed an accident where my cousin died right in front of me. That was traumatic, and that was one of the worst days of my life. Other than that, I hadn't experienced loss so close. My parents and others who were supportive of me and had witnessed my struggles and watched in worry, wondering if I would ever recover or die from this. They were there for me. They always were all my life. They knew my potential and watched, saddened as I let it disappear. Four years into my Sobriety, everything changed--- Everything. First, my sister's husband died unexpectedly, leaving her with their two boys and in poor health from her Diabetes. He was the brother-in-law that had gotten sober in AA and stayed sober for 17 years. Sadly, like so many, he once again thought it had been long enough. He went out, drank, and used, then struggled for five years to find his way back before he died from complications of his addiction. Two years later, my wife's mother passed away from a stroke. She had lived with us for our children's entire lives, and they were devastated too. One year later, my dad had a stroke, and my sister's health deteriorated. Then my mother got sick. We lost my sister, My Mother, and My Father in one year. We adopted my sister's two boys and have four teenagers in the house. I was named Trustee of my sister's and my Parent's affairs and had to take over a business with my brother. Really? Could I handle all this?

Everything changed. Except there was one thing that didn't. I stayed Sober through it all. If not for miracles but for the Grace of God, we carry on.

I tell you of this tragic series of events to tell you that Sobriety in life and through life, as hard as it may be, is possible, even for the worst of us that fall into addiction. I had built back Trust from my family that had lost it years before. I built confidence in them that I could manage their affairs. Through all prior knowledge of my past, they believed in me. When the time came to step up and do what was required and necessary for my family, I was sober, ready, capable, and willing. It was only possible because I was sober. Not once during or since did I ever think of numbing myself, even at the saddest time dealing with grief or the most stressful time dealing with the responsibilities. If I had chosen to drink, it would have been a shit show disaster of epic proportions. But I didn't, and I never wanted to, I believed I wouldn't, and did what I had to do not to. Which was still to focus on each thing and each step in front of me and on to the next. I don't share this to pat my back or gain praise. It is to stand here in Gratitude for what was freely given to me by God and other people along the way. It is a miracle, and I can't express enough that you can have it too.

Now that we want it, believe in it, and are willing to work for it, decide to do what is necessary, don't drink or use and have the patience to receive the miracle for yourself; what now?

Let's continue.

7

NOW THAT WE ARE PATIENT, ARE WE THERE YET?

You may have noticed that I have not discussed in depth the Familiar 12 Steps that are the foundation of A.A. and the many recovery groups that I have experienced and that have helped countless people recover from the affliction of addiction.

This is not because I don't believe in them or don't intend to address them.

Contrarily, I think there are lessons in them and lessons in the Big Book of Alcoholics Anonymous that are useful and applicable to everyone, not only alcoholics or addicts. One doesn't have to fit a specific profile to benefit from good information, universal human truths, and wisdom that may help us as people with addictions or as humans in general.

For an addicted person, specific stories in The Big Book will inspire you to say - that is me or that was me. I am almost sure of that, and I know I did.

I have waited to touch on the steps intentionally. I suffered from the instant gratification syndrome early on in my Recovery. I just wanted to get it over with, get people off my back, and move on. Even when I read the steps, I resistantly went along with it, listened to or ignored this or that. I did not live these principles even though I was going through the motions. I wanted part of it and believed some of it. I didn't work much at it or decide it was for me. My initial cluelessness about the importance of the prerequisites I stated here as a necessity for any of it or anything else to work is why I wanted to lay the foundation with things that might help you under-stand that you must want the Good Life that sobriety and these principles can give you. I did it Backward. I just did a bunch of stuff without sufficiently wanting it, believing it, or working for it. Until I did, it was just a prolonged, somewhat futile exercise besides the hard-earned wisdom. I learned a lot from it, so I am here to share it with you.

I mentioned many things people do that make them feel better and enthusiastic in the early phases of Recovery. Many things, such as exercise, eating well, sleeping better, taking on hobbies, and other things, will be great as we go through this journey.

These are all essential. Keeping connected with others and not isolating is also crucial. As long as we don't think jumping into these things will make life perfect, solve all the problems, and make the obsession, our past, regrets, resentments, or other issues that got us here immediately disappear, it's all good. Just be aware of the "Pink Cloud" syndrome and take it slow and steady.

Sometimes people will replace their obsession with alcohol or drugs with a habit or obsession for something else, like exercise, and they think they will sweat everything out and be cured. We might become physically fit but not in any way spiritually or mentally healthy. It is essential to be healthy in all these ways.

Focusing on positive rather than negative things like obsessing about not drinking is good. It is like the adage telling someone NOT to think of a pink elephant. The more you try NOT to think of it, the more you think of it. We don't want to obsess about NOT drinking even though we don't want to drink or use. It is much more effective to focus on what we can do, what one step or one good thing we can do. Once we gain confidence in things we can do, we will feel better, feel possibility, feel some accomplishment, and obsess less about the negative things we can't do or the negative things we have done. It gives us hope and makes Recovery less of a matter of depriving ourselves of things we think we need that were never positive or improving our lives at all. When we see how something that initially seemed like a burden enhances our lives, we will see the possibility of this Good Life ahead and believe we can have it. We can have it.

It is essential to replace old bad habits with new ones. Replacing hanging around dangerous, shady places with a more positive environment is vital. Avoiding toxic friends and relationships, detrimental to Recovery, that will only bring you down is also crucial. If you get anxious, nervous, or feel guilty about any situation, place, or person, it is not worth the rest of your life to act on the temptation to return to such scenarios and situations. If you keep doing the same things once again, you will keep getting the same results and the same shitty prizes. I know this can be hard. We can say, yeah, but Izzy, the drug Dealer and Sparky Magoo, that lives in his mom's basement and hasn't ever had a real job, have been my friends since kindergarten. They're alright if you get to know them. Hmm. Maybe so. What have you gotten that is positive and encouraging from this relationship? Are they where you want to be in five years? Exploring things may reveal they may be willing contributors to why we are where we are. If we are all going to make changes together and encourage each other; great! If they will bring you down, it's best to move on. We must make hard but necessary sacrifices, and we must make changes.

If we are aiming for a new life, we need to have a new attitude, a new perspective, new thoughts, new actions, and a new purpose. This purpose might be one we had once believed in that has been pushed aside, not forgotten but abandoned, and deemed no longer in our grasp due to addictions taking over and commanding our full attention, crushing our self-image. We may no longer believe we deserve or can attain such lofty goals.

We must change our view of ourselves. The habit of negativity and a poor self-image has been driven into our minds by listening to lies, not excusing our wrong actions, or releasing accountability for them; however, we can change. Often, we base our self-image on what others tell us and how they may see us in our addiction. We may hear that we are worthless, or we will never change. Some may have been called all sorts of terrible names that are recorded and repeatedly played back in your minds. We base our self-image on the lies we tell ourselves about what we deserve or can achieve. The Summit of the mountain seems an impossible, distant, and unreal place for us now, so we don't even put boots on to take the first step. The isolation and lying awake at night with thoughts coursing through our minds let the enemy paint the grimmest and most hopeless future for our life. It is all lies. When our minds and reasoning are clearer and we begin to take steps in the right direction, it is amazing how our outlook will change. We will realize all these negative thoughts were lies. We need to replace these thoughts with truth. God did not create us to be like this. We were born as a gift of hope, potential, and possibility that at one point went astray, but we can return and find our purpose again. I am not simply recommending "positive thinking" schtick that gives false hope. It is the truth. I have been in the depths of dark, negative thoughts and repeating erroneous judgments of myself. Anything I was thinking in those moments has been proven wrong with positive change, action, and consistent progress- not just "positive thinking," expecting spectacular results to appear magically with no effort on my part. You will realize the truth when you keep moving in the right direction.

The truth is that we can do anything we want and achieve anything we will set out to do if we stop accepting the lies and make the changes necessary, which will replace those thoughts and change the course of our life to a more happy, humble, content, and joyful, sober life.

Side Note: One of the things I have loved to do since I was a teenager was to write. I liked to write stories, poems, and songs and even had Ideas for movie scripts.

While I have written things here and there over the years, I am only writing with intent and true belief now. Wow, I'm even writing this book, my 1st one ever. Years ago, shivering, staring at the ceiling, unable to sleep in a hospital bed, I never imagined that would happen. I knew I had a story but never thought I would write it. Once, I did, but not anymore at that time. Only now am I pursuing many of these things that I have always wanted to do but still needed to have the will, determination, confidence, or patience to do in the past. I could not do them before; I stopped believing I could do them. I started feeling I couldn't, would never do it, and would relent to the fact that it wasn't for me. What changed besides not drinking? Everything. I believe in possibility. I believe in what I can do, not what I can't do, and I believe in potential and purpose.

Making new habits, becoming open to new ideas, meeting new friends, and establishing healthy relationships take time. Some of us spend a lifetime establishing these bad habits and tendencies, and we need the patience to create new ones.

They say it takes 21 days to replace an old thought with a new one or an old habit with a new one. I only partially agree with this regarding Recovery, however. We have been forming these things for quite some time, and they may have been dug in deep.

A few weeks might be long enough only to begin forming new ways of thinking, routines, and habits. Don't expect to be fully transformed, healed, and reach the Summit in a matter of weeks. Since we are doing it one day at a time and step at a time, we'll focus on that, we will get there when we get there and rejoice when the Miracle happens. It will happen if we do that one good, productive thing each day and don't drink or use today. Rinse, repeat.

HALT

There is an acronym that we use in Recovery. H.A.LT. It stands for Hungry, Angry, Lonely, and Tired. You might think oh, fun, we get to do word games.

Yes, we use a lot of acronyms in Recovery. It's not really a game, but there is nothing wrong with having fun. It is a good way to remember things. H.A.L.T., represent things that are very dangerous in Early Recovery.

HUNGRY

It is amazing how imbalances in our body, mind, and patterns can affect our thoughts, motivation, outlook, and mental health. I am sure you have heard of Hangry. I am sure you have felt it. When we are hungry and need fuel, if we aren't aware of or neglect this essential requirement, we are pushed back into the need for instant gratification. We need food, and our bodies will flip out unpredictably if we don't get it. We can get headaches, feel weak, hallucinate, get Hangry or super angry, and even pass out in the extreme. It is an imbalance, a lack of necessary nutrients, minerals, glucose, or water. I witnessed this to the extreme with my sister and her diabetic reactions. If a diabetic's blood sugar and insulin aren't regulated, they can go into a complete diabetic response, making the unknowing person think they are on drugs or psychotic. It was frightening to see her like that as a kid and not know what to do. The body is a complicated machine. If we don't think about watching our nutrition and fueling our body, we can become vulnerable to mood swings and all kinds of things that may make us do things we shouldn't and that are not helpful to our progress. We need to be aware of these things. We may not have even felt it in the same way when we were loaded because the alcohol or drugs were taking the place of what we needed in a very destructive way.

ANGRY

We can get Angry for any number of reasons besides the Hangry version. Have you ever heard of the idea that Anger is the enemy? It is. There are many frustrating, seemingly unfair things in this world and things to get disappointed and discouraged about. We can get frustrated and angry when things don't go our way, or someone says something we don't like. Anger really is the enemy. Regardless of what it is caused by, getting angry rarely solves problems. We often manufacture our own Anger with thoughts, often by developing scenarios in our mind that haven't even happened or aren't even true.

I can't count the times that I have been upset with someone for some perceived wrongdoing. It may have been about work. I literally pictured and played out the argument I was going to have with them over and over, assuming what they would say and how I would react. It was going to be heated and may come to blows. Then I saw them; they came up and said - Hi, good morning, how are you? What? W.T.F.! My whole scenario and plan diffused and deflated because they were nice. I had a plan. My mind was so shocked that I forgot what the argument was about. I wasn't angry anymore. It was B.S. I created that scenario based on lies and assumptions. Have you ever done that? I bet you have. Anger is the enemy, and assumptions are its accomplices. They can utterly mess things up. We must begin to distinguish between what in our mind is true and lies and assumptions. Take a moment, take a deep breath, and ask yourself, is this true, or am I making it up? What is the evidence that it is true? Is it all based on assumptions? Then don't create a scenario in your mind as if it already occurred when it has not happened and is not real. When we base our whole lives and how we react to them on lies and assumptions, we might be angry ALL the time, and then WE will be the enemy to others and not improve our lives.

LONELY

Now, many times I like to be alone. It can be peaceful, we don't have to please anyone, and we can relax. Read. Watch something WE want to watch instead of competing. Sometimes it is lovely.

Being lonely is different than alone. Lonely is involuntary; lonely is alone and longing for something or someone. We can be lonely because we feel nobody wants to be with us. We can be lonely because we are afraid to be around others. We may think we pushed them away, and maybe we did. Lonely is longing and painful.

When we are in Recovery, Lonely can be dangerous too. Alone with our thoughts can be a scary place to be. As they say, our minds are a tough neighborhood, don't go there alone. It is also a big test of our character and resolve. It's what we do when nobody is looking that tests our progress and stability. It took me quite a while to be honest about that part.

Our goal is to be confident and not fearful about being alone. However, it is a crucial part of Recovery not to isolate. We need to keep in contact with others who know what we are going through, hold us accountable and understand, and help keep us from listening to lies our minds will love to tell us. That's why it is important also to go to meetings or groups where we can share what we are going through, and some people will relate. Riding this out alone in the early days is not a prudent plan of action if we want to improve our lives. Trust me; I tried it many times.

For those of us that persevere, listen, and keep working at it, immediately or eventually, we usually look forward to meeting with these people and usually make some good friends in the process.

TIRED

When we change our ways and seek Recovery, it is a life-or-death situation, or at least our lives have been so negatively impacted; we must change course and are usually exhausted. We are tired of the struggle. We are tired of the problems; and we are sick and tired of being sick and tired, as they say. We are tired of disappointing people and ourselves. We are Tired. We will improve if we take the steps in the right direction.

In Recovery, Tired can be dangerous. Sleep deprivation can do many terrible things to our psyche and attitude. Sleep has been such a problem for so long, and the absence of the poison we got used to only worsens it. We often have trouble sleeping for some time, but it gets better. Once the chemicals are out, after we get some rest and at least some positive thoughts start replacing the negative, it will improve. Many natural sleep aids can help. I will not recommend anything specific because I am not a doctor, and everyone has a different constitution and things that will work and some that won't. Chamomile tea is never a bad thing. Look up homeopathic sleep aids or ask a pharmacist.

The period, however, where we have trouble sleeping is another opportunity for the enemy of negative thoughts, desperation, and hopelessness to try and derail our progress.

We must be patient; another good adage to hold on to and believe to be true is "This too Shall Pass." It will pass if we have patience, perseverance, faith, and resolve to move forward.

I cannot say it enough; you must stay on course and realize it will take time but know things will improve. There will be a day you will be the real you again.

Journaling your progress is not only part of the 12 steps of Recovery we will soon discuss; it is a great way to focus on positive progress, assess how one is doing physically and mentally, and keep our mind occupied with efforts and actions that will help us through.

Reading is also a great thing. Reading positive stories of victory, affirmations, and reminders of the truth to counter the lies and negativity that sometimes flood our minds is very beneficial.

8

DO NOT DISTURB:
TRANSFORMATION IN PROGRESS

Recovery was a long journey for me. It took so long to accept that I could have allowed myself to become dependent on something that seemed innocent, at first felt good, and that seemed to make things better and more fun. It helped numb feelings, and it loosened inhibitions. I thought it made me the person I was supposed to be. Eventually, it took me farther and farther from who I was. I was running numb in the opposite direction of the person I was or meant to be. There were times I felt I could never find my way back.

It is truly baffling and unfortunate how outside forces and a dangerous inside job in our minds so adversely influence the perception of ourselves, our potential, and our hopes for the future. No matter what our story, whether it began with a happy childhood full of hope, wonder, and excitement or it began with hardship, fear, and struggle, there was one point that most of us were innocent, happy children learning our way in this world and looking forward to things. Everything was new. Usually, there is less stress than in adulthood when we have set a particular course and begin to have responsibilities and accountability. We didn't worry as much.

Before we became addicted, we did have a different perspective of the world, another image of ourselves. The worse it got; our perception changed. Our outlook is sadly not a positive one when we get to what we call a bottom, and our confidence defeated. We may believe we have ruined our life; we can never get what we once wanted or go where we once enjoyed. We worry and become obsessed with thinking of the worst outcomes of every situation. We can't perceive the positive development in our current state.

Have we become different people? Do we no longer want or deserve happiness? Why, because of mistakes? Are we other people than those who once had hopes and dreams and maybe even believed we could reach them?

No, we are not. It is only circumstances that have changed. We may never get out of bed if we base our happiness, hopes, and dreams on current or past circumstances. Circumstances can change. They have over and over in our lives and will again. First, we cannot base our happiness on our circumstances. If we are going to become content, we must find peace as much as possible in any circumstance. We must believe that "This too Will Pass" even when the circumstances are good. They can always be better. We will also face challenges again. We must find the Joy within ourselves and the ability to be content in all circumstances before we can share it with others and craft it into a new life of optimism and progress.

Do you ever remember having a crush on someone when you were young? You thought it was Love. If You couldn't turn that picture of a heart with their name on your folder in class into a full-blown relationship forever, beginning in Middle School, you may as well not live. Maybe it wasn't that desperate, but some took that too far. But, more times than not, in five years, you don't even remember that person because now you have a crush on someone else. In 10 or 20 years, you may run into that person and say - Oh, Thank the Lord I did not date or marry that person, yikes! We had the strongest, seemingly deepest feelings, and yet, in time, they dissipated like the mist. That is why relationships and Love is not a feeling we have; it is a commitment we make to someone or something over time.

If we base relationships on a feeling at any given moment, they will -Never- last. It is the same with Recovery; it is a commitment over time, not a crush. You must commit to working at and loving your Recovery.

When we have found ourselves having the deepest, darkest, negative feelings about a circumstance that is happening right now, we must pause, breathe deeply, pray, meditate, and convince ourselves to realize the truth; it is only a circumstance. It is not fate, and it is not immovable or unchangeable. The hurt we may feel now is even more substantial than when we got rejected by that crush. This, too, shall pass.

We lie in fear and worry, making assumptions and setting conclusions about things that have not happened, from which we can change course by our own choice and action. We can put towards a new path. All we must do is stop lying there listening to lies and take these first steps on this new day towards progress and then do it again another day after that.

I want to share another well-known Acronym. It is T.H.I.N.K. When caught in a negative mindset, we think negative thoughts about ourselves and may take our frustrations, resentments, and anger out on others. Often it will be someone who has nothing to do with why we are angry or frustrated. The people closest to us usually take the worst of our wrath. This Acronym, T.H.I.N.K., reminds us to pause our thoughts before we speak and ask these questions.

Is it **TRUE**
Is it **HELPFUL**
Is it **INSPIRING**
Is it **NECESSARY**
Is it **KIND**

T.H.I.N.K. before we speak.

The first one might be the most important, as if something isn't True; it most likely isn't Helpful, Inspiring, Necessary, or Kind. If based on a lie, it will not have lasting value and will inevitably cause harm to ourselves or others. Suppose we aim to change negative thoughts and actions towards healing, honesty, integrity, and a more positive outlook and life of Joy and contentment. In that case, we must be more discerning in how we communicate. We pause and think about our intent and the effect of what we say to ourselves and others before we speak. In that case, we can avoid perpetuating negativity, conflict, adverse reactions, regrets, or resentments if what we say is not Truthful, Helpful, Inspiring, Necessary, or Kind. We are often reactionary and too anxious to get a word in, debate what someone says, argue to prove our knowledge, disparage theirs, or prove we are right. If we T.H.I.N.K. first before we speak, we will find it is better to hold our tongue, be quiet and composed and Let it Go. We undoubtedly will reap the rewards of more peace and less conflict with this strategy in thought and communication.

Worry, Anger, and fear never did anything positive for us, so why do we want to hand everything over to it? You can have this Good Life full of promise, possibility, productivity, contribution, contentment, and Joy, and you can stay sober and Love it.

I promise. Thinking and communicating more intently and positively will help our progress.

Even when we try and stumble, we only fail when we don't get back up. The intent here is never to spew some flowery, feel-good, positive-thinking smoke into shady places. I will tell you positive thoughts without action will get you nowhere. A positive effort, commitment, and belief can get you anywhere. Lying in self-pity will not change our lives except for the worse, pulling us down into despair, false assumptions, and lies about us, telling us we are not worthy and incapable. It is all lies. It will not get anything back we have lost. The only way to disprove the lies is to prove them wrong, and that takes action, one day, one step at a time. Our family is patient with us, but they want us to change for the better, and it is up to us. We must be patient with ourselves but not wallow in regret, fear, and self-pity. If we want to change, we must take action to change. God is patient with us and will undoubtedly allow our circumstances to change. He does not want us to linger in this dark place. But he also wants us to change our hearts and minds, which will take commitment, perseverance, action, and prayer.

In review:

- We must want to change more than anything else.
- We must believe we can Change.
- We must decide to change.
- We must work at it, take action, and take the first steps to change.
- We must stay committed even when we make mistakes or fail.
- Failing one time or many doesn't make a failure. Not getting up does.
- Don't believe assumptions are valid or the lies are true.
- Circumstances are not destiny.
- There is a Power Greater than us that will help pave the way if we ask for it honestly and earnestly.

THE ACTIONS WE TAKE THE LEAD TO THE LIFE WE MAKE.

We Will Succeed- If we follow steps laid forth by wise people before us, stay humble, be patient, persevere, and know and believe that there is a Power Greater than us that will help us prevail if we are open, willing, and Honest. We must not let ourselves be a barrier to our possibilities and accomplishments. LET'S DO THIS!

9

THE TWELVE STEPS

AN OFFER OF SOBER LIVING MIRACLES

B ack in the early thirties, when there was not a widely known or followed program or method for helping someone addicted to alcohol to recover, they were often sent to hospitals or institutions and treated as if they were insane with no hope of recovery. They saw these people as those with no chance to return to polite society and be capable, worthy, or productive members of it.

In 1935 in Akron, Ohio, a man known as Bill W. met a surgeon, Dr. Bob S., who were both highly intelligent and, at times, very successful. They were also raging alcoholics that, at one point themselves, felt there was no hope for them but to die in an addicted hell of Alcoholism. They met through an association with a fellowship called "The Oxford Group. "This fellowship emphasized universal spiritual values in daily living." (A.A. Website) for people in general. A friend of Bill W. Had come to him one day, delighted at how he had "found religion" and quit drinking. Bill was intrigued. He later met Dr. Bob, who, on his own, could also not kick his affliction with alcohol. It was this meeting and association, along with their introduction to a theory by Dr. William D. Silkworth from New York that Alcoholism was a Malady of the Mind, emotions, and body, that began their Journey to work with alcoholics to help each other recover under the revelation to treat Alcoholism as a "Malady" or disease and not just a consequential destiny of poor choices by "bad people" with weak minds as it was sometimes before. They began to meet with other alcoholics and share their experiences, strength, hope, and success, and they started to achieve results. They developed the 12 steps, partially attained from Biblical principles of repentance and forgiveness, among others, and these spiritual values in daily living from the Oxford Group. These values and principles can apply to anyone. It was a miraculous revelation of how sharing hopes, stories, ideas, and similar life experiences with each other could change the hearts, minds, and lives of those suffering from addiction. They started Alcoholics Anonymous and based the organization on one of their traditions of attraction and not based on promotion for anyone who truly desires to quit drinking and change their lives for the better. The member must choose to seek help and follow these principles. There is accountability but not coercion. It is not a religious organization, but the focus and acceptance of the idea of a power greater than us that can help restore us to "sanity" are undoubtedly vital.

Since then, millions and millions of people have found sobriety and a new beginning and hope to adopt these principles into their lives. You can't argue with massive success.

Not believing that this organization or the principles shared by many recovery programs could benefit people was not my problem, and I saw that it had. I was not so naive to think that after millions had committed to it and recovered from Alcoholism or addiction, it was a scam. They weren't asking for money or investment to help some "recovery guru" get rich. The only investment is in ourselves, our time, and a commitment to ourselves and a better life through sobriety. We may chip in a dollar for coffee and some flyers, but there is no profit motive here.

It took me so long because of the ever-prideful and stubborn idea that I did not need it. I was not like these other people with the same story, with the same disorder. In my mind, I wasn't. I just got a bit of a habit, but I could surely figure out a way to quit it or at least significantly "tone down" my drinking. Such is the tragic affliction of denial for millions who cannot see this better life through the fog we have driven so far into that we cannot even see at all.

It is amazing how simple these things are when we finally actually surrender to the obvious, help and possibilities right in front of us, the idea that there is a higher power than us and people wiser than us that are offering to help us through it with the only payment or requirement being to say - yes, I am Ready. Life is not over, and the offer is Sober living Miracles and a better life for all involved. It is right here for us if we accept it.

Both AA and Celebrate Recovery have been a crucial part of my Journey. Everyone's path may be different while much the same. Much of my final progress to this point was seeded in the first beginnings of A.A. when some blessed wise people suffering from the affliction of alcohol addiction began to gather with each other, tell their stories and share their journey to a new and better life. It is the fellowship. It is meeting with others who know what you are going through, have been there, can relate, and will begin to have your back. It is gathering with those that relate after finally being honest that had the most significant impact on me. This fellowship with people that can relate to us can be experienced in many types of groups, not just AA. God, or our "higher power" will be there to help us as well. "Where two or more are gathered, there I will be in the midst." Mathew 18:20

You are not alone in this. For me, all these people along the way, even those I couldn't relate to, even those that were annoying, even those that were still in denial like me, even those that came in drunk or stoned, even those that failed again and again as I did, some returning and some never returning or even, sadly, dying, and certainly those that don't think just like me or believe what I believe, have all played a part in my journey. I am grateful that I always listened to that one thing and kept coming back. Sometimes it is that one thing that makes all the difference in the world, even if it takes as long as I to see the light and realize the miracle.

These steps are simple, but our minds make them complicated. Keep it as simple as possible. I will briefly break them down as I list them below.

I will never say one way is the only way to sobriety, as we see different variations and paths. However, these steps and these principles are full of wisdom, truth, and virtue and can help anyone make a positive change from wherever they are in life. For those addicted to alcohol or drugs, it is a well-proven way to a better life.

1. We admitted we were powerless over alcohol — that our lives had become unmanageable.

Here is where we aim to be humble when we commit to change. Some may take this pridefully and say, "I am not powerless over anything. If I set my mind to it, I can do anything." I love positivity, but this is a lousy start. It doesn't mean you don't and will never have power over anything. Let's try not to take things personally, face reality, and allow ourselves to say yes to improving our lives. If alcohol or drugs did not hold power over us, we would not be in some of the positions where we have gotten ourselves. In this state - what was simple can become overwhelming and difficult for us to accomplish, and to make progress, the way we live needs to be more manageable and sustainable. We must admit that to change our lives for the better and relieve this powerlessness and unmanageability.

2. We Came to believe that a Power greater than ourselves could restore us to Sanity.

It is incredible to what depths we will ride pride, ego, and arrogance against all evidence and justification to make us think there is nothing more powerful than us, nothing we can't conquer alone without help. The insanity that we must restore may include this false belief—undoubtedly, being restored in more ways than one is imperative. Unquestionably, there are countless things we have done and situations we have gotten into in service to addiction that have been utterly insane by any rational measure. I have described many of mine, and there are many more. A restored life of Sanity is, without question or doubt, a better place to be.

3. We made a decision to turn our will and lives over to God's care as we understood Him.

Here is where we sit down, be quiet, listen, and realize what we have been doing is not working and will never work again, and rest and Surrender are desperately needed. We are not giving up on life or throwing in the towel; it is more like when we were young, learning to swim. Before we knew how, we would trust our parents or teachers to keep us afloat, not letting us sink. We would sink if we tried to tread water and flap our arms and legs around, getting exhausted. They told us to be calm. We held our arms back, breathed, and floated, knowing they would hold us up. We need to let go. Close our eyes, take a deep breath, and float. Don't worry about swimming laps. Don't worry about solving all our problems. They will never be solved anyway while fighting, flailing, and sinking. That can only happen with Surrender. God will keep us afloat. First, we float, allowing ourselves to stop working so hard, flapping our arms, fighting, and flailing. When we are ready to swim, we will know. As we understand him, God will help us all along the way. What one's understanding of God or your "higher power" is will be revealed. Be patient. As we say, Let Go, Let God. This is Surrender.

4. We made a searching and fearless moral inventory of ourselves.

Here is where we search our minds, heart, and soul for the true nature of why we turned to escape. Who hurt us? Who did we harm? What is our part in all we have experienced or suffered? What do we need to admit or get off our chest? What repentance is due. Who do we need to forgive, not allow resentment to control our mind and life, and stop "drinking poison waiting for someone else to die"? What truth do we need to explore and learn? The truth really will set us free. We take this out of our minds and hearts and put it on paper into the light, not to be public but to be released from us.

5. We admitted to God, ourselves, and another human being the exact nature of our wrongs.

Here, the burden of stuffing feelings, thoughts, resentments, regrets, pain, sorrow, sadness, secrets, and longing is released, honestly, into the light, perhaps for the first time in our lives. It may be our first time quietly speaking these things to anyone. I have known those who have kept painful secrets for years and decades, only being able to heal when they could finally reveal and let them go. These captive secrets only keep us in bondage and are the origin of many of our hurts, habits, and hang-ups that keep us from realizing the content, happy life of joy and sobriety that is possible. We may even think we hide secrets from God by not saying them aloud, acknowledging the truth, or holding ourselves accountable for our part. Have you ever held on to something so tight and been ultimately relieved to let it go even though it was hard? You will be grateful for this moment. It is Catharsis, and finding someone we trust to listen and be there with us for this achievement is essential.

6. We were ready to have God remove all these character defects.

Sometimes we are blatantly aware of doing things we should not be doing. We know there are things we do that hurt others. We know that there are things that do not make our life better. We are not bad, but we grow so accustomed to our ways that we are unwilling or afraid to change. "I don't do the good things I want to do. I keep doing the evil things I don't want to do." Is it working for us? Is it making our lives better, holding on to defects and old habits? There comes a time we must stop fighting, living in fear, and proving the definition of insanity repeatedly. When we can confess that we are ready, this is that time. We must be willing to cut out the things and defects in our lives holding us back.

7. We humbly asked God, of our understanding, to remove our shortcomings.

When we are ready in step six to admit our failures, defects, and shortcomings, we don't just make an admission of our flaws and think we are stuck the way we are with no way out.

We must believe we can change and have faith that if we want it and humbly ask God, he will wash our defects and shortcomings away to make way for a new life.

8. We made a list of all persons we had harmed and became willing to make amends to them all.

We looked at our life in the inventory we explored and developed in step four. Undoubtedly, we recalled quite a cast of characters. Each of these people is part of our story. Some of them may have felt hurt by our actions or words in some way. In every instance we recall that we harmed another, we admit how we may have hurt them. We hold ourselves accountable for that hurt. We agree to make amends personally and symbolically when we cannot in person. Our willingness here coincides with our verbal and mental commitment to ourselves and God to hold ourselves accountable for our past actions.

9. We made direct amends to such people wherever possible, except when doing so would injure them or others.

Our goal here is to take responsibility for the harm our past behavior or actions may have caused another person. It is to hold oneself accountable humbly and sincerely and acknowledge it to the other person in apology with genuine remorse. While we may be hopeful in healing and reconciliation for past hurts, we don't ask for forgiveness nor express any expectation of it. It is a heartfelt offering left to them to accept or requite as they will. We must accept that forgiveness may not come in this circumstance, and we may be unable to reconcile relationships.

If our presence or attempt to contact, speak to, or visit any of these people would cause more harm or resentment, we will not harm them to make us feel better. We offer our apology earnestly in spirit, hoping and praying God may deliver it somehow. We make this action step toward acceptance, accountability, and repentance, not expectations of the desired result.

10. We Continued to take personal inventory and, when we were wrong, promptly admitted it.

Since we are approaching this Journey one day at a time, focusing on the present moment and taking action to address the challenges and opportunities that arise each day, it is essential to reflect on each day as a measurement of progress and to approach the next day with a fresh perspective towards improvement. Journaling or assessing our day and our steps to quickly realize and acknowledge where we can improve is a valuable way to help us stay present and move forward. We recognize and admit if we were wrong in our actions or words and resolve to make progress and improvement in this area.

11. We Sought through prayer and meditation to improve our conscious contact with God, as we understood Him, praying only for knowledge of his will for us and the power to carry that out.

Here we are adopting new practices, strengthening our spiritual connection with a higher power than us, or God as we may understand this to be. It is to be present with prayer and meditation, seeking positive change through awareness and understanding of our purpose and God's will in our lives.

12. Having had a spiritual awakening as the result of these Steps, we tried to carry this message to alcoholics or addicts and practice these principles in all our affairs.

When we see what living these principles and becoming aware of the new hope and possibilities presented before us can do and truly feel the change in our spirit and lives, we are not to hold onto it secretly and selfishly. One of the most significant, fulfilling, and substantiating benefits and gifts is to help and serve others humbly and with gratitude, as did those before us. They say it is better to give than to receive. Many will say that helping others afflicted with addiction helps them as much or more than the ones they will help. I know this to be true.

Thus, we can be grateful for the new life given to us but also rejoice and find joy in helping others to achieve this new Good Life of belief in possibility, of desire to do what's right, of diligence to keep working, of commitment to staying sober and living these principles in all areas of our lives, being honest, forgiving, slow to anger, peaceful, content, joyful and sharing this belief and possibility as best we can with others that are ready and willing and in need.

The Twelve Steps | Alcoholics Anonymous. https://www.aa. org/the-twelve-steps

FEATURES AND BENEFITS

LOVING SOBRIETY

L oving Sobriety is a journey that requires commitment, dedication, and patience. Making needed changes in our life can seem like a complete overhaul; in many ways, it is, from the inside out. In ways, we are becoming new people. Yet, in other ways, we are just returning to the person God made us and willed us to be and the person we have always wanted to be, not living in fear, regret, and resentment without confidence, courage, or belief that we are worthy to live a life of happiness, contentment, and Joy while being Sober. We can begin Living and Loving with Honesty, Integrity, new clarity, and focus, without fear, regret, and resentments, being more authentic, caring, and less self-serving while genuinely Loving ourselves again.

When we take the first steps, make this commitment, believe in ourselves, and trust in God, we can be the person he meant us to be and decide to change, the rewards are immeasurable, and the feeling of pride and self-love that comes with it is a wonderful thing to experience. Significant change is not easy, but it is the most worthwhile and fulfilling investment we can make in ourselves, our families, and our future.

One of the most significant things about loving Sobriety is the feeling of control it gives us. Addiction can make us feel powerless, in fear, constant worry, and out of control, but choosing to live a sober life is an act of self-empowerment. It shows that we are in charge of our life, setting our course intently, with Courage, Strength, Willpower, and Faith to overcome challenges.

Another beautiful thing about living and Loving Sobriety is the clarity of mind and more strength and steadiness of body. We have more stamina and energy. Without the haze of drugs or alcohol clouding our thinking, we can see the world with a fresh perspective. We can make better decisions and accomplish more things we grew to believe were no longer possible and are now possible. We can focus on our goals and enjoy the beauty of life in a more profound and meaningful way.

I recall the days when doing the simplest things became burdensome, difficult and stressful. I was unsteady, weak, and overwhelmed at the thought that this would be life for me. I was in disbelief, I had gotten to this place of weakness, fear, regret, and sadness, not knowing, or believing in a way out. There is a way when we start with the one step, the one good thing we can do today, and build confidence to do it with progress, not perfection the next day.

The fight and the struggle will dissipate. Feeling overwhelmed will settle into quiet, humble confidence and being self-assured as we progress one day, one step at a time, with patience, perseverance, and growing support from good people and true friends who genuinely want to see us prevail.

Loving Sobriety will help us to build healthier relationships with those around us. Substance abuse can damage relationships, but Sobriety allows us to repair those relationships and form new, healthy connections. We can learn to communicate more effectively, listen better, T.H.I.N.K first, and be present now, leading to more authentic and fulfilling relationships.

Furthermore, Loving Sobriety means pursuing our passions and hobbies with renewed enthusiasm and joy. We have more time, energy, and resources to focus on what makes us happy and fulfilled. We can find joy in the simple things in life and discover new interests that we never knew we had, and we don't get to dream of them wishfully; we can do whatever we decide and resolve to do. We could start a non-profit, build a business, volunteer, spend more time with loved ones and family, travel, write a book, make a movie or even more important, be proud to work towards something positive, serve others and have a purpose. Everything is possible when we live and Love in Sobriety and Faith.

Sometimes we will believe we will miss out on things when we are Sober, an irrational fear based on assumptions, habit, and chronic avoidance of being present. We think there is always something more fun or thrilling away from wherever we are or someone having more fun than us. We are so used to drinking and using being the focus of every activity we may struggle to see ourselves having fun or enjoying anything without it. Undoubtedly, we miss a lot more because of drinking and using than we ever will being sober. Many activities were so focused on the substances and getting loaded that we missed or didn't remember many of the details if we remembered them at all. I can't count the number of events where my friends or I were not even watching games, concerts, or other forms of entertainment because we were in line for the booze or sneaking away to get it, so we could "better enjoy" the event we were missing almost entirely. As addiction progressed, any event just distracted us from what we really wanted: to drink or use. For some, the F.O.M.O. (Fear Of Missing Out) may have even turned into F.U.N.A. (F@$K#D UP Naked and Arrested). That never happened to me, but I hear it is not uncommon nor fun. We will Love enjoying and appreciating all kinds of fun and entertaining events and making memories that we will actually remember afterward and for a long time when we grow and learn to Love Sobriety.

Here are some things I guarantee we won't miss about living loaded and in our addictions.

We won't miss living in constant fear.

Fear and worry can be a constant burden in our addiction. We worry about our health, family, relationships, and how we will get the next fix or drink. When or if we drive, we worry about the law, getting arrested, and losing freedom and money. We worry about accidents and harming others or ourselves. We worry about the future. We will Love Sobriety for relieving much of this fear and worry.

We will not miss being extremely unhealthy, constantly feeling sick, exhausted, and weak.

In our addiction, we inevitably neglect health as the priority of getting drunk or high reigns supreme. We do an incredible amount of damage to ourselves. Despite horror stories of liver disease and failure, high blood pressure, poor nutrition, diabetes, not eating or sleeping well, clouding our mind, killing brain cells and ability to think straight, we believe, "not me, I feel fine, I'll work out, eat something and be good to go. Maybe some year I will go to the Doctor." Our body will Love Sobriety for sure.

We will not miss our clouded, confused, overwhelmed, and uncertain existence in addiction.

Let us be honest; even when we believe we know what we are doing, we do stupid things when loaded. It is perilous. We make bad decisions and often regret them. We act compulsively without "playing the whole tape." We are reactive without thought of consequences. We jump into situations thought-lessly, pay the price, and receive unwanted, often ridiculous prizes for misjudgment, recklessness, and stupidity. Clarity will be a welcome reprieve and a glorious blessing when we grow and learn to Love Sobriety.

We will not miss letting ourselves and others down, ruining relationships, and feeling constant disappointment in ourselves or directed towards us.

It is a certainty that relationships suffer when we are in our addiction.

We may know we love others and make promises to change, but our affliction holds the wheel and makes all the turns. Addiction breaks up and ruins families, friendships, and how we treat and communicate with those we love in the most negative ways that sometimes can never be reconciled. Our families, friends, and those we interact with will Love our Sobriety when we become honest and earnestly pursue it without unrealistic expectations of others.

We won't miss spending or losing all our money and constantly wondering where it went.

The amount of money and resources we will expend in the unrewarding, black-hole financial disaster of addiction is absurd, startling, and tremendous. Our families, future, and ability to invest in them, it and ourselves will Love the financial makeover of Sobriety. We will now have more resources to invest in a better life and future for ourselves and others and enjoy life more thoroughly.

We will not miss feeling unworthy, hopeless, depressed, and incapable.

One of the most critical aspects of finding Sobriety is learning to love ourselves. Many people who struggle with addiction have low self-esteem, making it difficult to believe we deserve a better life. Sometimes this is a shock because we were so much more vibrant, confident, and hopeful before becoming enslaved to addiction. However, through recovery, we learn to accept ourselves for who we are, flaws and all. We learn to appreciate our strengths, work on our weaknesses, and discover that we are worthy of love and happiness.

Sobriety also brings a sense of peace and contentment that is hard to describe. We have more time and energy to focus on what truly matters when no longer consumed by addiction. We can form healthy relationships, pursue our passions, and experience the simple joys of everyday living. We can make choices that align with our newfound or recalled values and beliefs when cravings, irrational impulses, or poor decisions no longer control us.

These changes can lead to a happier, healthier, more fulfilling life of hope, possibilities, and Joy when we Love Sobriety.

Reflecting on the journey chronicled in this book, I am grateful for, and still moved and inspired by, the incredible transformation that can occur when we face our addiction head-on and commit to a path of Sobriety. The journey is challenging, requiring courage, honesty, and a willingness to confront our deepest fears and insecurities. But as we travel down this path, we discover a new sense of purpose, appreciation for life's simple pleasures, and a new capacity for love and compassion.

The Twelve Steps and the Sober Living Miracles that we will experience and that I have outlined in this book offer a roadmap for this journey, but ultimately, each of us must find our way. We must be willing to take ownership of our past mistakes and shortcomings and embrace the possibility of a brighter future. We must be patient and kind with ourselves but also committed to the hard work of recovery.

As I close this book, I am eternally grateful to God for his Grace, the many people who have supported me along the way, and the opportunity to share my story with others who may be struggling with any form of addiction. I hope this book will offer inspiration, guidance, and hope to those on their shared but unique journey toward Loving Sobriety and that it will help break down the stigma and shame that often surround addiction. We are not alone if we have the courage and faith to reach out to another willing hand to guide our first steps, knowing God will be with us as we continue to grow in strength, wisdom, and love as we move toward a life of contentment and joy. God's Grace, these steps, and the support of others have manifested for me more than I could have imagined years ago, and I hope this for all who face these challenges.

May God of your understanding Bless you on this journey to Loving Sobriety.

SHARE THE JOY OF WANTING, BELIEVING AND TAKING ACTION TO EXPERIENCE A SOBER LIVING MIRACLE

You now know the importance of setting sobriety goals and working towards them, even if this involves stepping outside your comfort zone.

Simply by leaving your honest opinion of this book on Amazon, you'll show other people the importance of taking that first step as they make their way to the summit of a happy, fruitful, meaningful life.

LET'S HEAR FROM YOU!
IF YOU ENJOYED THIS BOOK, PLEASE LEAVE A REVIEW TO HELP OTHERS

Thank you for your help. You can encourage other readers to accept their powerlessness over addiction, find vital sources of support, and shine a light for others who may have lost hope in the miracle that lies within them.

Please leave a brief, honest review ASAP when you complete the book. It would really mean a lot and will spread the message of hope for others too.

EPILOGUE

ONE PRAYER TO GO PLEASE

We used to recite this Prayer at the beginning of those first morning AA meetings I attended. While it took a long time to sink in, this Prayer stood out as one of those "Seeds" implanted in my heart that would eventually grow. I recall that I printed it on a picture of a beautiful sunrise.

I took it when I got up early to attend one of those meetings. What wonderful things we notice as we begin to see clearly. I still have that picture, and I still think this Prayer is profound, and these are inspiring words to aspire to and live by, so I'll leave them right here for you.

Prayer of St. Francis of Assisi (Prayer for Peace)

> *Lord, make me an instrument of your peace:*
> *where there is hatred, let me sow love;*
> *where there is injury, pardon;*
> *where there is doubt, faith;*
> *where there is despair, hope;*
> *where there is darkness, light;*
> *where there is sadness, joy.*
> *O divine Master, grant that I may not so much seek*
> *to be consoled as to console,*
> *to be understood as to understand,*
> *to be loved as to love.*
> *For it is in giving that we receive,*
> *it is in pardoning that we are pardoned,*
> *and it is in dying that we are born to eternal life.*

(Prayer of St. Francis of Assisi (Prayer for Peace). https://www.cathedralstm.org/about-our-catholic-faith/expressing-our-faith/treasury-catholic-prayers/prayer-st-francis-assisi-prayer-peace/)

Made in the USA
Middletown, DE
23 December 2024

68125166R00077